FOOD LOVERS'
GUIDE TO
CHARLESTON & SAVANNAH

Help Us Keep This Guide Up to Date

We would love to hear from you concerning your experiences with this guide and how you feel it could be improved and kept up to date. Please send your comments and suggestions to:

editorial@GlobePequot.com

Thanks for your input, and happy travels!

FOOD LOVERS' SERIES

FOOD LOVERS'
GUIDE TO
CHARLESTON
& SAVANNAH

The Best Restaurants, Markets & Local Culinary Offerings

1st Edition

Holly Herrick

gpp

Guilford, Connecticut

Editor: Amy Lyons
Project Editor: Lynn Zelem
Layout Artist: Mary Ballachino
Text Design: Sheryl Kober
Illustrations © Jill Butler with additional art by Carleen Moira Powell and MaryAnn Dubé
Maps: Trailhead Graphics Inc. © Morris Book Publishing, LLC

ISBN 978-0-7627-6012-1

Printed in the United States of America

All the information in this guidebook is subject to change. We recommend that you call ahead to obtain current information before traveling.

Contents

Savannah, 153

Recipes, 209

Appendices, 231

About the Author

Holly Herrick is a Cordon Bleu–trained chef, national award-winning food writer and restaurant critic, and longtime Charleston resident and booster. After stints in Paris, Minneapolis, and Jackson Hole, Wyoming, Herrick landed in Charleston, where she worked for seven years at *The Post and Courier,* Charleston's only daily newspaper, before leaving to focus on her freelance career in 2006. That same year she received a First Best Place Award for Newspaper Series, Special Sections, and Special Projects from the American Association of Food Journalists.

Her work has appeared in *Bon Appétit, Gourmet, Southern Living,* and several regional publications. Her column, Delectable Delights, appears regularly in *Lowcountry Living Magazine.* She is the author of *The Southern Farmers Market Cookbook, Charleston Chef's Table* (Globe Pequot Press), and *Tart Love—Sassy, Savory, and Sweet.*

Acknowledgments

Aside from the great chefs and beautiful cities of greater Charleston and Savannah, huge thanks to the following persons: My intrepid assistant and scout, Lucie Norvell Maguire, who reminded me how old I am with her computer wizardry and astounded me with her absolutely fabulous nose for good food and reporting about it. Oh, and she does maps, too. Thank you, Lucie. I am pleasantly obliged to thank the wonderful folks at the fabulous Catherine Ward House Inn, where my dog Tann Mann and I stayed for most of our Savannah research. Thank you, ladies, for welcoming both of us with open arms, despite our sometimes tattered, road-worn state. Leslie Larson and Marianne Preble, you are the best! This team works up the best breakfast this side of Texas, hands-down. As always, love and thanks to my family and sweet friends from my quiet little street in Charleston and elsewhere for your emotional support. May all of you find great food and great times whenever possible, for that really is the delicious stuff that makes life worth living. Bon appétit!

How to Use This Book

During the long research and writing of this book, the greatest inspiration came from these beautiful, foodie-fecund cities themselves. Just 110 miles apart, both Charleston and Savannah are poised on the banks of the sea-soaked Lowcountry, a salty swath of marshes, estuaries, and waterways that stretch along the coast between both cities and a bit beyond. Both share ample larders and long colonial and antebellum histories. Yet like fraternal twin sisters from an old, eccentric Southern family, each has emerged with distinctly individual culinary personalities and perspectives. This book is dedicated to these fine cities and the chefs, residents, producers, and markets that help polish, refine, and embellish their respective gustatory renown. Thank you, thank you, thank you, one and all!

I worked and ate my way for 6 months through both cities with a most discriminating palate and at my own expense at every pass.

It was daunting at times, from a caloric, energy, and budget perspective, but I got there and had a grand time doing so! My goal was to find the essence of both cities and to present to you the best places and where you could enjoy them. I hate the idea of anyone tramping about Charleston or Savannah, spending money, and missing the best foodie targets. So, voilà, *Food Lovers' Guide to Charleston & Savannah* presents herself. Dig in and enjoy!

Food Lovers' Guide to Charleston & Savannah is divided into two parts: Charleston begins on page 1 and Savannah begins on page 153. Each listing shows the name of the establishment, address, phone number, and website (when available) and each chapter is made up of different sections, including Foodie Faves, Landmarks, and Specialty Stores, Markets & Producers.

Food Events

Anything food related, from food and wine festivals to beer and ale tastings are included under this category. Many are annual or semi-annual events that are not to be missed when you're in town.

Foodie Faves

These are restaurants favored by lovers of good food and drink where you're more than likely to see a lot of local fans and even the occasional local chef. Perhaps less renowned than "Landmarks," this is none-the-less the type of place where you're most likely to experience the broadest range and personality of each city's everyday dining choices.

Landmarks

Every city has restaurants that have carved a special place in history and in collective culinary hearts as a true landmark. Charleston & Savannah are no exception. These are restaurants where maverick chefs from many different restaurant eras (some going back 50 years or more) have blazed trails that simply cannot be ignored and in many ways, define Charleston & Savannah's destination dining.

Specialty Stores, Markets & Producers

From perfect pastries to exotic spices and carefully crafted ale, this is an important food area that has exploded within the past few years. In this section, we list the best, what they do best, and (when applicable) the best times to visit.

Learn to Cook

Charleston and Savannah are full of generous culinary genius and afford several venues—from cooking schools to culinary tours—to learn more about cooking and these cities whether you're visiting or if you live here. Here's where to find them.

Price Code

We also included price information for restaurants using the following scale system for a single entree:

$	Less than $10
$$	$10 to $20
$$$	$20 to $30
$$$$	More than $30

Recipes

The recipes included in the Recipes chapter (p. 209) either reflect Lowcountry tradition or are simply outstanding and impossible to resist. All are clearly and simply written with sensitivity towards the needs of the home cook. Enjoy!

Appendices

For your convenience we've included in the appendices an Index of Eateries by Cuisine and Index of Purveyors found throughout the book. Additionally, there is a general index that follows the appendices.

Charleston

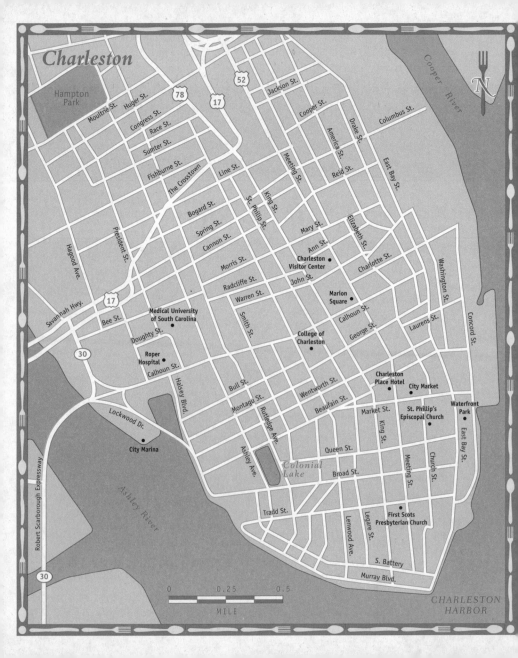

Introduction

It's easy to wax poetic about Charleston, though not as beautifully as Charleston native DuBose Heyward (of *Porgy* fame) did in his haunting, lyrical ode to Charleston. In "Dusk," written in 1922, Heyward most correctly described Charleston, also known as The Holy City, as "alone among the cities."

She is indeed entirely unlike any other and to know her is to love her, except possibly in August when oppressive heat and humidity threaten to temporarily strip the heartiest bloom off even the most ardent rose.

What's not to love? The peninsula itself is swaddled by a scenic network of waterways and swaying marshlands and embraced by the glistening waters of the Cooper and Ashley Rivers (which Charlestonians like to say "meet to form the Atlantic") just beyond the harbor jetties. Days begin and end with the tolling of the bells from the 200 churches that dot downtown, a glorious audible testament to the city's founding charter that mandated religious tolerance. Antebellum and Colonial homes stand regally throughout the city as gorgeous, visual reminders of Charleston's 300-plus-year history that has withstood hurricanes, fires, earthquakes, poverty, and war.

Still, every spring unfailingly ushers in the heady perfume of wisteria and jasmine blooming while fall and winter annually translate into convivial oyster roasts and blazing open fires in country fields. Ranked as the nation's most polite city for over a decade by *Travel + Leisure* magazine and populated with a mere 125,000 residents, Charleston is a pleasant place to live and to visit, to say the very least.

It's also entirely delicious. Though once revered by tourists (some 4 million streamed through in 2011) first and foremost for Charleston's well-preserved history, it runs neck and neck in recent years with cuisine as a principal reason to come calling, according to annual visitor profile studies by the Office of Tourism Analysis at the College of Charleston. This is an apt stat, since food and history are inextricably linked to the present (and the future) of dining and eating in Charleston. The extreme breadth, wealth, and sophistication of early colonists from Europe, Barbados, and later slaves from Africa, combined with an abundance of local foods from a verdant land and teeming sea, formed the ingredient list (okra, grits, fowl, oysters, shrimp, etc.), practicality, and prowess to create bedrock Charleston staples like she-crab soup and shrimp and grits. Carolina Gold rice, the stuff behind Charleston's huge wealth (surpassing that of all other American Colonial ports at her financial peak in the late 18th century) was and still is stirred into fragrant stews, rice puddings, and pilafs.

Now, at the rosy, breaking dawn of a new decade, Charleston's chefs and producers are looking back to Charleston's well-preserved past to find the award-winning culinary path to her present and future. Home now to three consecutive James Beard–winning chefs (Robert Stehling of Hominy Grill in 2008, Mike Lata of FIG in 2009, and Sean Brock of McCrady's in 2010) and the fifth best food and wine festival in the 2011 BB&T Wine + Food Festival, according to *Forbes Traveler,* she's well on her way.

Farmers' markets, once a rarity, are springing up and growing up all over town and country, offering assorted produce, artisanal cheeses, grass-fed meats, homemade pickles, freshly baked breads, and Southern pies. Once confined to downtown, landmark restaurants showcasing artisanal meats and heirloom vegetables are equally at home in Mount Pleasant as they are on the more remote barrier islands. Chefs' collective battle cry of "local, local, local, and seasonal too" has grown even more  focused on conscientious sourcing and growing practices. Many chefs grow and nurture their own gardens, while a brave few such as Sean Brock of McCrady's nurture not only heirloom seeds but also their own heirloom pigs. Specialty shops, particularly a plethora of adorable bakeries serving Paris-worthy perfection and handcrafted beers and ales are de rigueur when only 3 years ago, they were virtually nonexistent. And, mixologists are swizzling and muddling their way through a tasty mix of pre-Prohibition era drinks at snazzy joints like The Gin Joint, Husk, Charleston Grill, and restaurants all around greater Charleston.

Charleston is my adopted home. Like so many have done before, I fell in love with her at first sight and have watched her grow from the rather gangly, beautiful culinary teenager she was in 2000 when I moved here to the stunning, graceful gustatory beauty she is today. In the past 5 years, a new wave of talent has raised an already high bar to diz-zying heights of diversity and perfection—these days you can't walk 10 feet in most parts of downtown without coming across a tasty temptation.

Since 2000, I've had the honor and pleasure of writing about Charleston as a restaurant critic and cookbook author. On a near daily basis in researching this book and other assignments over the years, I've spent most days anonymously sampling food (that I pay for) at Charleston restaurants and specialty shops, combing farmers' markets, or reading about new hot spots and I've spent the other days writing about them. In this book, I include only those places that are worthy of any serious foodie's time or money. Who can afford to waste either, especially in a city as lovely as Charleston? If it's not in here, more than likely I don't think it's remarkable, or, less than likely, it's opened since this book was published.

Getting Around

Because peninsular Charleston, particularly the restaurant-rich section below Calhoun Street (see pp. 19–60), is so exquisitely beautiful and relatively small (encompassing just a few square miles), it is without a doubt best traveled by foot, if at all possible. Meandering along the alluring streets and alleys ensures free, unexpected views of luscious gardens, ancient architecture, and quiet neighborhoods you would otherwise not enjoy if traveling by almost any other means. Watch your footing, however. Cobblestones and sidewalks tested by time can be challenging and are best treated with respect and comfortable walking shoes.

The second best choice for covering peninsular ground is a pedicab, also known as a rickshaw. For a relatively easy price, a party of two can be whisked through the streets on a small, comfortable cart, usually fueled by the strong, attractive legs of a male College of Charleston student or recent grad. They're also a nifty mode of transportation when your evening entails libations that may make driving dangerous. Make your reservations in advance and await handy door-to-door service and a cooling, windy good time. I recommend Charleston Rickshaw Co., www.charlestonrickshaw.net.

Charleston, for reasons good and bad, is not a great taxi town. In my experience, service is often unreliable and taxis, especially when you are walking down the street in need of transport, are very

hard, if not impossible, to hail. In this way, Charleston is no New York! However, there are exceptions to every rule and the **Charleston Black Cab Company** (www.charlestonblack cabcompany.com) is one of them. A highly reliable fleet of black London-style cabs, they are easy to spot, and dependable, especially for getting around peninsular Charleston and back and forth from the airport, which is about 15 minutes from downtown. Time pick-up cab reservations must be made in advance.

The **CARTA** bus system is difficult to navigate, especially to get to and from restaurants. The Trolleys (DASH) provide free transport around downtown Charleston and look like the 20th-century trolleys that used to run on tracks through the city. For information on routes and times for either, visit www.ridecarta.com.

Once you start navigating higher up on the peninsula, particularly above the Crosstown (Highway 17), restaurant and food destinations are fewer and farther between, though still commandingly delicious. Getting to them, and also to other towns in greater Charleston like West Ashley or Mount Pleasant, requires covering distance and bridges that mandate travel by car, unless you have a very big taxi budget. Car rental businesses are prevalent throughout the area, with the easiest access at the Charleston International Airport in North Charleston, about 15 minutes from downtown. Outside of downtown Charleston, parking is (mostly) easy and accessible. Downtown, respect meters and signs. If you don't, you will be ticketed, booted, or towed, especially in high-traffic tourist areas like the Old City Market and the French Quarter. The Charleston Visitor Center is an excellent resource for information on the many public parking alternatives downtown (www.charlestoncity.info).

Keeping Up with Food News

With Charleston's explosive food scene, it seems I learn about something new every day, sometimes several times a day. Be it a new chef, a new restaurant, a new concept, a new market manager, a new location—the list goes on and on. While it's exciting, it's frustrating to try to stay current especially since that's a big part of my job. Fortunately, there are some reliable information resources out there, both online and in print. The *Post and Courier,* Charleston's daily newspaper and the South's oldest newspaper, provides restaurant and food news in various sections, including the business section. The most complete foodie fodder can be found in Thursday's Charleston Scene section, which includes restaurant reviews, restaurant news, and interviews with chefs and bartenders. The *City Paper,* a weekly, creates a restaurant guide  every spring and fall called *DISH*. The paper provides ample restaurant coverage and is released every Wednesday. *Charleston* magazine is a beautiful monthly magazine that includes restaurant reviews and food news and does an annual food issue every December. These resources can also be found online at the following addresses:

www.postandcourier.com
www.charlestoncitypaper.com
www.charlestonmag.com

There are additional websites and social-media resources that can be helpful for obtaining food news for greater Charleston, including my own blog (visit www.hollyherrick.com and click on "blog") and Twitter posts (my handle is @HollyHerrick). The blog is mostly about Charleston and Savannah restaurants, and I visit and update it often. Marion Sullivan, the food editor for *Charleston* magazine (listed above) is a knowledgeable food professional and prolific tweeter, averaging at least three to five daily tweets about breaking restaurant and food news around town. Her handle is @mbscooks.

www.scsfa.org: The South Carolina Specialty Food Association is dedicated to spreading the word about the best specialty products produced in South Carolina on this informative and well-managed site.

www.dinesc.com: This website breaks down South Carolina regionally and by city to help visitors find the type of food and environment they're looking for in a dining experience. Very easy to navigate, it's a useful starting point, but far from complete. It also includes information on the Hilton Head and Beaufort area closer to Savannah.

www.charlestonrestaurantreviews.com: Again, a decent starting point for doing broad searches according to the type of restaurant you're looking for. The site provides star rankings, websites, and other useful information.

www.culinarycharleston.com: An excellent and complete resource for finding restaurants and their sites. It also provides foodie vacation packages and Charleston foodie news.

Food Events

BB&T Charleston Wine + Food Festival, www.charleston wineandfood.com. This is *the* Charleston destination event of the year for all serious foodies, no matter where they're from. The festival draws thousands from around the country and the world, and has been deemed one of the top five food and wine festivals in the United States by *Forbes Traveler.* Huge chef and food celebrity names like Daniel Boulud, Danny Meyer, Bruce Aidells, John Besh, Alexandra Guarnaschelli, Tom Colicchio, Sara Moulton, Tyler Florence, and Bobby Flay have graced the festival's myriad stages, and the list gets bigger and brighter every year. A slew of extreme local chef talent helps flesh out one very tasty food and wine menu. These 4 days and nights of food fun kick off the first weekend of March, ushering in spring's active tourist season. Events vary every year but usually include restaurant dine-arounds, wine and food tastings, chef cooking competitions, farm to table field trips, and all things delicious. The core events take place on Marion Square in the heart of downtown Charleston. Tickets sell out early and can be purchased from the festival's website listed above. A 501(c)3 non-profit organization, the festival has donated hundreds of thousands of dollars to local charities and culinary scholarships.

Charleston Mac-Off, www.charlestonmacoff.com. Southerners take their mac 'n' cheese very, very seriously. In Charleston, it's everywhere—from homey versions at casual meat 'n' three's to **Graze**'s (p. 105) lobster mac 'n' cheese to **Cru Cafe**'s (p. 26) sinful, four-cheese, bubbling, crunchy mass of cheesy goodness. Self-professed "mac-heads" get a chance to sample mac 'n' cheese from several local eateries and vote on their favorites. Wash it all down with beer, wine, and plenty of music. The event is held during the month of November, downtown at the Visitor Center Bus Shed. Proceeds go to a select charity. For tickets and information visit the website listed above.

Charleston Restaurant Week, www.charlestonrestaurantweek .com. Even dynamic Charleston has cyclically slow restaurant traffic during certain weeks in September and January. To help step up business and to introduce a wider audience to restaurants they may not otherwise visit for budgetary reasons, the Charleston Restaurant Association introduced the wildly popular Restaurant Week, which occurs twice a year and typically increases restaurant traffic by up to 75 percent. Close to 100 restaurants participated in the program in fall 2010, and Kathy Britzius, director of the Charleston Restaurant Association, anticipates that number will continue to grow. Restaurant Week showcases a series of prix-fixe menus with three courses for $20, $30, or $40, making it prime time to graze your way through some of Charleston's best for less. The website is easily navigated and quick links direct readers to the menus of each participating restaurant.

Grace Episcopal Tea Room, 98 Wentworth St., downtown; (843) 723-4575; www.gracechurchcharleston.org. OK, so it's not an official food event, but unofficially, this is one of the most quintessentially Charleston experiences imaginable. It takes place just 11 days of the year (starting on Memorial Day) when Charleston's spring is in full, fragrant bloom and Charleston Spoleto USA, a premier art festival, is in full throttle. Church ladies (and gentlemen) create an abundance of delectable staples like sweet tea, shrimp salad sandwiches, and crab soup, most created from old Charleston family recipes. The gorgeous dessert tray creates a virtual buzz as it travels, by gloved hand, around the gingham and floral draped church hall and luscious, surrounding gardens. Attendance and indulgence here are signature rites of passage for locals and visitors lucky enough to know about it. Tickets are purchased at the church door and proceeds have raised thousands for select area outreach programs for decades.

The Lowcountry Oyster Festival, www.charlestonrestaurant association.com. Yet another wildly popular fund-raising event for the Charleston Restaurant Association, the world's largest oyster festival definitively kicks the blah out of winter while celebrating the briny goodness of the Lowcountry's celebrated mollusk—the Eastern oyster. There is a whole lot of slurping going on at Boone Hall Plantation through the spirited oyster-shucking and oyster-eating contests. Local chefs provide alternative goods at the food court, while live music, beer, and wine keep the mood light. Kids will enjoy the Kids' Corner, a jump castle, and pony rides. The festival has been named one of the top 20 events in the south by the Southern Tourism Society and for nearly 30 years has been a much beloved local food event. For tickets and information, click on the link on the association's website.

Southern Living Taste of Charleston, www.charlestonrestaurant association.com, www.southernliving.com. For more than 30 years, this family-friendly, annual fall event has attracted thousands for a day of food and fun. It has two warm-up events on the days prior to "The Taste," beginning with an Iron Chef competition held at the **Culinary Institute of Charleston** (see p. 87) and a Taste of the Arts along Broad Street, downtown. The Southern Living Taste of Charleston itself is a 2-day affair that is held out at sprawling, scenic Boone Hall Plantation in Mount Pleasant. Nearly 50 fine dining and casual restaurants participate as guests stroll and nosh on sampler plates and sip beer and wine. *Southern Living* magazine brings exhibits, cooking demonstrations, and guest editors and writers to the table. There are pony rides for the kids and trolleys for the weary to get back to the parking lot when the fun is done. Proceeds from the event go to select charities such as The Ronald McDonald House, cancer research, and Charleston-area education/schools. Click on the link on the site above for dates and tickets.

Supper Clubs

Guerrilla Cuisine, www.guerrillacuisine.com. Charleston's very first underground supper club, Guerrilla Cuisine got its start in 2007 because owner and longtime area Charleston chef "jimihatt" wanted to "start a buzz." The way it works is simple. Jimihatt contacts prominent local or visiting chefs (or they contact him) and they set a date and a time for a dinner. Jimihatt spreads the word, largely through social media, to would-be attendees. Those who sign up and prepay are sent the address of the event via email about 2 days prior to the actual dinner. Venues have ranged from warehouses to airplane hangars to boat docks and have been as intimate as just 21 attendees to 100 or more. "We showcase local chefs, musicians, artists, and local farmers," says jimihatt. Not only one of the hottest tickets in town, the events (and there are roughly 24 dinners a year) are for a good cause. Participating chefs select a charity and donate a percentage of each dinner's proceeds accordingly. The average price for a dinner is about $75. For more information and to purchase tickets, visit the website listed above.

L.I.M.E. Charleston, www.limeincharleston.com. Trinidad native, chef, and owner of L.I.M.E., Renata Dos Santos takes "liming" seriously! In her homeland, liming—or hanging out with friends and family usually with food and beverages—represents a relaxed, happy outlook on life. L.I.M.E.'s acronym synthesizes what the supper club stands for: Local. Impromptu. Moveable. Evening. Like Guerrilla Cuisine, the location is released just 2 days before the event. L.I.M.E supports local resources in a big way and mandates that chefs (all Culinary Institute of Charleston or The Art Institute students or local grads) use at least 25 percent local products, but Renata says most use close to 100 percent. Chefs accommodate special requests for vegetarian, vegan, gluten-free or allergen-free meals. Chefs also choose a charity for each event. Menus range from 7 to 9 courses and cost $125, all inclusive. Each dinner has a different theme. Recent dinners have featured entertainment as diverse as belly dancers to the Oscar Meyer Wienermobile. Tickets and reservations can be made on the website listed above.

Because everyone always asks me "What are your top favorite restaurants/meals/food & drink spots in all of Charleston?" I'm going to go ahead and, somewhat reluctantly, list them here. I say "reluctantly" because this list, like the Charleston food scene, is dynamic and by no means constant. So, this short list is, of course, subject to change. However, the establishments in this short list are included because they consistently deliver exceptional food, style, and personality panache in such a way that I (and many others) consistently yearn for yet another visit to each of them. Please keep in mind that everything included in this entire book has been chosen because it is already considered exceptional and visit-worthy. This list is not listed in order of preference—one is as delicious as the next.

The Charleston Farmers' Market (Peninsular Charleston Above Calhoun Street), p. 85

Charleston Grill (Peninsular Charleston Below Calhoun Street), p. 42

Peninsular Charleston Below Calhoun Street

Downtown Charleston is indeed a peninsula of land bordered by two tidal rivers, the Ashley and the Cooper, named after two of the Lord Proprietors of the original colony. The peninsula gets broader and deeper above Calhoun Street, before it finally gets swallowed by land and reaches over the waterways to neighboring communities forming greater Charleston.

The land that extends south of Calhoun Street comprises the area that most people think of when they think of Charleston. Dotted with stately old mansions, gracious parks, water fountains, and the tolling bells of countless ancient churches, it includes the bustling College of Charleston campus and the cherished enclave known as South of Broad, the place where the "S.O.B.'s" live, if you believe this jocular nod to Charleston high society. Restaurants and eateries comingle beautifully with the neighborhood ambience and are very concentrated, so getting to them by foot is a cinch, especially between Calhoun and Broad. Below Broad Street is exclusively residential and eatery-free (except for the private Charleston Yacht Club), so build your appetite with a morning stroll along the Battery and bring it a bit uptown for lunch or dinner (or dinner and supper in Charleston-speak!) at one of the many, many wonderful choices available here.

Foodie Faves

Amen Street, 205 E. Bay St., downtown Charleston, SC 29401; (843) 853-8600; www.amenstreet.com; Seafood; $$. Amen Street is one of my favorite places to go to eat when I want really fresh, local, and beautifully prepared seafood, especially for lunch, which Amen Street does especially well. The inspiring name breathes new life into the former name of Cumberland Street (which flanks one side of the restaurant). Local lore says Amen Street was so-named because "amens" could be heard coming from neighboring churches. You'll say amen and hallelujah to Amen Street's impeccable setting, which showcases 19th-century exposed brick walls, gleaming, golden pine, and stunning chandeliers made from oyster shells and iron. Executive Chef Stephen Ollard (that's just one "C" shy of collard, folks!) is a talented disciple of good cooking and local seafood and only uses the freshest from local waters, including the Lowcountry's celebrated shrimp, flounder, and oysters. In season, the creamed corn that comes with the stellar fried seafood plate is not to be missed. Fresh fish of the day comes served with three refreshingly simple preparations that beautifully complement without muting the delicate flavor of the fish. A long bar and volume-muted television screens make for a tempting seat for a cocktail or glass of wine to go with one of Amen Street's most revered menu items, the delicious and whimsically presented shrimp corndogs, which come with tangy mustard and tiny, tart pickles.

Bakehouse, 160 E. Bay St., downtown Charleston, SC 29401; (843) 577-2180; www.bakehousecharleston.com; Bakery; $. Dynamic duo Matt Lewis and Renato Poliafito originally transported their sophisticated yet down-home style of baking (using distinctly American ingredients like Coca-Cola and Oreos) to Bakehouse in Charleston from their original shop ("Baked") in Brooklyn, New York. Career demands required them to sell the Charleston-based Bakehouse to locally based proprietors, but much of their original imprint remains unchanged, including the bright orange-and-white ceramic tile, the unique wildlife-inspired logo, and most happily of all, the iconic Sweet & Salty Brownie that has turned more than one head, including Oprah's and Martha Stewart's. This brownie is made daily and is unbeatable chased with a steaming cup of Charleston Coffee

Roasters rich, dark java. Individual tarts, cakes, cupcakes (consider citrus coconut!), seasonal pies, mini refrigerator pies (consider banana cream!), and brownies and bars flesh out one magnificent sweet menu, but there are also savory options offered in sandwiches and more during lunch hours. Clean, bright, centrally located in the heart of the restaurant row on this section of East Bay, Bakehouse is also Wi-Fi friendly and attracts a lot of laptops and their users.

Bin 152, 152 King St., downtown Charleston, SC 29401; (843) 577-7359; www.bin152.com; Wine Bar; $. "The Bin," as it's called by its myriad fans, is headlining the mini-restaurant renaissance taking place on Queen Street near King in the heart of the French Quarter. A pocket of a place that is part wine and cheese joint and part art and antique gallery, it's got huge heart mostly emanating from husband/wife owners, Patrick and Fanny Panella. Fanny is French and oozes sincere Gallic charm. Let her put together one of her artful displays of thinly sliced charcuterie, duck mousse, or buttery, cured bresaola paired with 1 or 2 of the house's 21 (many imported) cheeses while Patrick picks a pour from the 100-plus-bottle wine collection. The narrow tubes of chewy, dewy, ultra-fresh baguettes are sliced very thin and are eminently edible, especially spread with a warm, fragrant French Morbier or English Stilton. Awash in white bead-board and golden pine, The Bin is relaxed yet cosmopolitan and draws an assorted cast of well-behaved characters.

Blind Tiger Pub, 36-38 Broad St., downtown Charleston, SC 29401; (843) 577-0088; Eclectic; $. For years, the "BT" has become practically infamous for its sexy, ancient brick-walled patio and garden, hellacious late night partying, and post–wedding ceremony bashes. Food has always been a relatively small part of the equation until Chef Mitch Wyman stepped up to the plate here a few years ago. Formerly at **39 Rue de Jean** (see p. 82), Wyman borrows from that restaurant's mussels, burgers, and quiche themes, but gives them his own, rugged twist. For good measure, he throws in a whopper of a steak sandwich with caramelized onions, demi-glace, and a mountain of hand-cut fries dusted with crunchy sea salt. You can taste the French precision in his work, even if the surroundings are suggestive of a slightly high-end dive bar. The food and ambience make the Blind Tiger worth a visit, especially on a sleepy, hungover Sunday morning for an exceptional Bloody Mary and a crab cake with an authentic hollandaise.

Blossom, 171 E. Bay St., downtown Charleston, SC 29401; (843) 722-9200; www.magnolias-blossom-cypress.com; Seafood/ Southern; $$$. Blossom has changed its mind a few times about what kind of restaurant it wants to be, at one point it was mostly Italian and another, Southern. These days Blossom is mostly all about seafood with a Southern twist with some pasta dishes and a small selection of gourmet pizzas baked in a snazzy wood-fired oven thrown in for good measure. Blossom's restaurant sisters (all three are owned by the same restaurant group, HMGI), **Cypress** (see p. 44) and **Magnolias** (see p. 49) flank her on both sides and have received more praise, but Blossom shines strongly as a fine place for a quiet lunch or dinner amid comfortable, deep banquette seating, sophisticated yet whimsical decor, and a lovely courtyard for alfresco dining. Executive Chef Adam Close hails from Nashville and does beautiful, restrained pairings with locally sourced fish and produce in tempting dishes like pan-seared flounder with rock shrimp, creamy rice pirloo, and smoked-tomato butter; and pan-seared scallops with apple and celery-root slaw, Oyster Mushrooms from **Mepkin Abbey** (see p. 101), and Mustard Butter.

Bull Street Gourmet, 60 Bull St., downtown Charleston, SC 29401; (843) 720-8992; www.bullstreetcharleston.com; Deli/Grocery; $. If **Burbage's** (see p. 25) recalls the past, Bull Street Gourmet recalls the present in the form of the masses of students from nearby College of Charleston who flock to this gourmet nugget of good-ness for breakfast, lunch, and dinner. Actually, Bull Street Gourmet is recognized by foodies of all ages for its knockout sandwiches prepared with imported and domestic meats, specialty cheeses, and fresh bread that get all dressed up with the sophisticated

likes of walnut pesto for "The Mozz" and the cranberry mayonnaise that envelops its justifiably "famous" roasted chicken salad. Stunning soups are prepared fresh daily and there is always a tempting tray of chunky cookies on the counter right by the register for that final, irresistible, point-of-purchase moment. The grocery/deli also stocks a vast array of very well-priced boutique wines and "small brewery" beers. A large, central wooden table and counters invite a leisurely lunch between classes, or they're happy to wrap it all up in their "Good to Go" fashion for an afternoon picnic in one of the many lovely parks in this quiet residential area of Harleston Village. Bull Street Gourmet just added a second, much larger location at 120 King St. near the intersection of Broad Street, downtown. Owner Justin Croxall has expanded the menu, kitchen, wine, and beer selection and is offering meals to go as well. See Bull Street Gourmet's recipe for its **Famous Chicken Salad** on p. 211.

Burbage's, 157 Broad St., downtown Charleston, SC 29401; (843) 723-4054; Deli/Grocery; $. The more things change, the more it seems we want them to stay the same. Burbage's serves up heaping doses of nostalgia and delicious eats that satisfy heart and soul with old-fashioned simplicity. Kids come for candy after school and the Burbage brothers even keep a credit ledger for regular customers. Mr. Burbage, now retired, bought this house at the corner of Broad and Savage in 1961 and it's been operating as a corner deli and grocery ever since. His sons Al and Matt run the ship these days and consistently produce delicious egg salad, shrimp salad, and pimento cheese sandwiches served on soft, white buns. House-made soups like Brunswick stew, chili, and split pea and ham and slow-cooked barbecue infuse the little white house with the big green awning with delicious aromas all day long, every day, except for Saturday and Sunday when it's closed, just like the good old days.

Caviar & Bananas Gourmet Market & Cafe, 51 George St., downtown Charleston, SC 29401; (843) 577-7757; www.caviarand bananas.com; Deli/Grocery; $. Another husband-and-wife team, Margaret and Kris Furniss operate this gourmet dream come true just a few doors down from **Patat Spot** (see p. 36). They left corporate America and New York to start their dream here in Charleston and it comes in the form of this gleaming white and stainless steel one-stop gourmet shop, and you can eat here, too.

A clear glass case, pregnant with 60 prepared dishes from sky, sea, and earth, takes center stage. Choices here are as earthy as meat loaf and exotic as Asian chicken lettuce wraps. A slew of sandwiches, sushi, and salads are prepared at several different stations. In the middle and all around, you can find domestic and imported best-quality cheeses, charcuterie, and yes, caviar and bananas. Sweet-tooths are satisfied with a tower of fresh baked goods and old-fashioned candies, including Charleston Chews. See Todd Mazurek's recipe for **Broccoli & Lentil Salad** on p. 213.

Cru Cafe, 18 Pinckney St., downtown Charleston, SC 29401; (843) 534-2434; www.crucafe.com; Eclectic; $$. This pale, butter-hued wooden house with a beautiful, sunny porch is a long-standing preferred Charleston dining destination. Executive Chef-Owner John Zucker graduated first in his class from Le Cordon Bleu, Paris, which affords some of the very best training available. Situated on the corner of endearing Motley Lane, Zucker would be the first to tell you he likes to mix things up in his kitchen, drawing ingredients from Asian, Thai, and Hispanic pantries as well as classical French and Italian larders. He insists on top quality ingredients and applies them to sensual dining delights like a duck confit arugula salad and Cru's celebrated Chinese chicken salad, a crunchy garden of crisp carrots, red peppers, daikon, and fried noodles all wrapped up in a snappy fresh ginger dressing. Don't even try to resist the restaurant's four-cheese macaroni and cheese, which showcases tender orecchiette pasta coddled in bath of oozing, nutty cheese topped off with bread crumbs and broiled to order. The menu changes seasonally and affords a broad selection in both small-plate and entree portions at gentle prices—same goes for the wine and craft beer selections. Select outside seating on pretty days and allow passing horse-drawn carriages to lull you into a sleepy, Charleston state of mind.

Dixie Supply Bakery & Cafe, 62 State St., downtown Charleston, SC 29401; (843) 722-5650; www.dixiecafecharleston.com; Cafe; $. This diminutive cafe doesn't look like much from the outside. It's tucked between a gritty looking L'il Cricket and the edge of the heavily trafficked tourist area of South Market Street and its requisite tourist-trap eateries. Don't be deceived by Dixie's exterior. Inside, it's warm, cozy, and familial. Co-owner Allen Holmes' family roots run 300 years deep in Charleston and most of the recipes used here come from his family's recipe file, as interpreted by Executive Chef Patrick Woodham. Dixie thinks and does everything big—big portions and big Southern flavors. Breakfast is served all day and includes a stellar version of shrimp and grits that's generous with the bacon and the shrimp. Sandwiches stagger with the weight of their hefty fillings and the tomato pie is the stuff of legend—so much so the recipe is top secret. Dixie's comes layered with fresh basil, thinly sliced tomatoes, oodles of cheese, and sweet, spring onions in fresh pastry, all served from a very deep dish with a chunk of sweet-potato cornbread for added flavor. There is comfortable seating out-side when weather allows. See Dixie Supply Bakery & Cafe's recipe for **Shrimp "BLFGT" Sandwich** on p. 215.

East Bay Meeting House Bar & Cafe, 160 E. Bay St., down-town Charleston, SC 29401; (843) 723-3446; www.eastbaymeeting house.com; Wine Bar/Cafe; $. Someone once said you can't be all things to all people. Well, East Bay Meeting House is thriving doing just that. Its urban, dark-wood good looks spill outside through large, sunny French doors, and tall windows have cobble-stone views of quaint Gendron Street at the corner of East Bay. By morning, it's a light-bite break-fast spot serving quiche, yogurt, and fruit, with a Bloody Mary or a Mimosa from their perfectly polished top-shelf bar, or a frothy cappuccino or vanilla latte—take your pick. Come midday, lunch is served, and from 4 to 11 p.m. look for tasty tapas and sexy sandwiches. Adult beverages are as expertly mixed as the coffee, and are best enjoyed while taking in the beautiful artwork on loan from nearby local galleries. Small and intimate yet spacious and comfortable, East Bay Meeting House attracts an eclectic, young-sophisticate crowd from morning to night. Monday evening features Open Mic Blues & Poetry and Happy Hour runs from 4 to 7 p.m., Monday through Friday.

Fleet Landing, 186 Concord St., downtown Charleston, SC 29401; (843) 722-8100; www.fleetlanding.net; Eclectic; $$. Pick any one of Charleston's many sunny, warm days to take a seat at The Fleet. Panoramic views of the Cooper River, the harbor, and front-row seats before the regal Arthur Ravenel Jr. Bridge (one of the largest cable-stayed bridges in the world) will command your attention, even as you are digging into Fleet Landing's sturdy, seafood-intensive fare. Formerly an abandoned World War II US Navy Debarkation Station, these days Fleet shines with beautifully appointed nautical themes, friendly service, and a general feel-good mood. On Sunday, it is a frequent destination for families seeking post-church sustenance, and it also is a popular watering hole for the young professional set. An open-air deck full of picnic tables and umbrellas is a perfect perch to dig into Fleet Landing's especially delicious shrimp and grits, gigantic stuffed hush puppies, fried-seafood baskets or luscious lump crab-cake sandwich. Ample, free, and easy parking, a rarity downtown, is offered in front of the restaurant. Take advantage of it while you can. Fleet Landing fills up fast during peak hours, especially on those especially beautiful days.

Gaulart & Maliclet, 98 Broad St., downtown Charleston, SC 29401; (843) 577-9797; www.fastandfrench.org; Cafe; $. Those in the know eschew the more complicated French name of Gaulart & Maliclet and opt instead for this little French cafe's nickname: Fast & French. In existence for over 25 years, Fast & French's enduring appeal has as much to do with its bohemian, beret-toting, black-clad clientele as with the Gallic charm of French natives/owners Gwylene Gallimard and Jean-Marie Mauclet, and their reasonably priced and reliable food. *Chien chauds* (hot dogs) on toasted baguettes and ample layers of Dijon mustard go down with wine, water, or a cool microbrew—there is no Coca-Cola on the menu. Fondues are silky smooth and laden with wonderfully stinky, flavorful French cheese and daily fresh soups and sandwiches are de rigueur here. Seating is at high countertops on high stools. Be prepared to get to know your neighbor. Fast & French fills up fast for *déjeuner* around noon.

The Gin Joint, 182 E. Bay St., downtown Charleston, SC 29401; (843) 577-6111; www.theginjoint.com; Eclectic; $$. The 1920s come roaring back with a swizzle and a sling at The Gin Joint. Owners Joe and MariElena Raya set up shop here less than a year ago to sate the growing thirst for authentic, old-fashioned cocktails made with love, prime liquors, mixers, and care. MariElena is the daughter of Charleston culinary legend Robert Dickson, who ran a very successful restaurant in this same space for 3 decades. After he retired last year, she and her husband completely transformed the formal dining restaurant into a highly respectable and delicious "joint" where gin "drink(s) proper" and folks "speak easy." A very talented chef and CIA grad in her own right, MariElena cringes at the thought of canned anything (especially whiskey sour mix!) and creates some amazing food to go with the amazing drinks Joe mixes and muddles at the busy bar up front. Try the irre-sistible sweet, spicy, rich Korean pork buns, which come on pillows of milky, chewy steamed dough, or dig into a fancy Berkshire hot dog dressed up with truffles and caramelized onions. The Gin Joint also offers a lovely assortment of imported cheeses and an abbreviated "Sugar" menu that's packed with ingenuity in delights such as *foie gras* "M&M's" and frozen carrot cake. It's impossible not to smile at the handsome servers sporting suspenders and bow ties while raising a retro-martini glass to thirsty lips. Cheers!

Hank's Seafood Restaurant, 10 Hayne St., downtown Charleston, SC 29401; (843) 723-3474; www.hanksseafoodrestaurant.com; Seafood/Southern; $$$. Hank's, with its pine-plank floors, chocolate leather booths, white linen tablecloths, and dim lighting, feels very much like a man's man kind of place. Situated in an early 1900s ware-house near (but not too close) to the Market Street area so heavily traveled by tourists, it was designed to imitate the art of a classic, retro fish house long recalled by owner Hank Holliday. Seafood plat-ters featuring mountains of mollusks and other gleaming seafood shimmer on beds of chipped ice that dot the landscape of Executive Chef Frank McMahon's domain. A talented Culinary Institute of

America chef with an impressive résumé, Irish native McMahon puts his stamp on some of the best seafood available in Charleston. His focus is fresh and simple and comes through clearly in perfectly executed classic sauces and preparations that combine classic technique with imagination. A friend of mine refuses to order anything other than the roasted grouper with a sweet corn, leek, lobster and rock shrimp risotto topped off with a champagne citrus beurre blanc when he comes to town. Smart move! It rocks with flavor, but savor some of Chef McMahon's personally sourced local oysters with a refreshing mignonette sauce, and you may never leave your seat.

High Cotton, 199 E. Bay St., downtown Charleston, SC 29401; (843) 724-3815; www.mavericksouthernkitchens.com; Southern; $$$. Easy live music floats nightly from the animated bar at High Cotton, where a colorful crowd and well-poured drinks flow in abundance. Next door, the casually elegant and airy dining room with its slowly turning ceiling fans is always full of the fragrant aromas that drift from the active open kitchen. High Cotton serves the kind of food that used to be served at wealthy, Lowcountry plantations, like shrimp and grits and gumbo over Carolina Gold rice. Although it serves dinner nightly and lunch on Saturday, High Cotton is perhaps best known for its popular Sunday brunch, where the after-church crowd comes for plates stacked high with biscuits, eggs Benedict, and gargantuan, fluffy omelets. Light streams in from East Bay through huge, inviting windows, which make the space sparkle with congeniality.

Jestine's Kitchen, 251 Meeting St., downtown Charleston, SC 29401; (843) 722-7224; Southern; $. For three generations, nanny Jestine Matthews fed the Berlin family's bellies and hearts with expertly crafted Southern soul food, from fried chicken to sweet tea (which owner Dana Berlin Strange calls the restaurant's "table wine"). The long line that snakes around this restaurant every single day that it's open, combined with its central downtown location, might seem suspiciously like tourist bait. But, that it most certainly is not! People come from everywhere to soak up the generous spirit and hearty portions of delicious soul food here and have done so for over 15 years. Meals begin with cool refrigerator pickles and end with freshly made pies topped with freshly whipped cream. In between, dig into fried pork chops, meat loaf, stewed lima beans, and all-around goodness. Check out the quaint bakery around back after your meal, if you want to take some of Jestine's home with you to enjoy later. Jestine lived to be 112 years old, so you can toss the guilt and hope that this kind of food and fun will help you do the same.

Kaminsky's Most Excellent Dessert Cafe, 78 N. Market St., downtown Charleston, SC 29401; (843) 853-8270; Desserts; $. It took friends visiting from out of town to turn me on to the unique pleasures of Kaminsky's, which delivers the kind of sweet-tooth punch no sugar junkie could possibly resist. Having long ago written it off as a tourist trap, I was delighted to discover, rather late in the game, Kaminsky's refreshing late-night goodness and eye-popping display of assorted cakes, tarts, cookies, and pies in the massive front-counter display. Desserts are made daily and refreshed throughout the day to feed the noon-to-late-night masses. The place is regularly packed with after-dinner dessert seekers and also offers a full wine, beer, and liquor selection, along with kid-friendly steamed milks, floats, sundaes, milk shakes, and dessert martinis.

Marina Variety Store Restaurant, 17 Lockwood Dr., downtown Charleston, SC 29401; (843) 723-6325; www.varietystorerestaurant .com; American; $$. An old-school, greasy-spoon diner meets saltwater views at this Charleston classic that's been family run and owned since 1963. It's sandwiched between the scenic City Marina and a filling station and oozes with stick-to-your-ribs goodness. Good ol' boy locals congregate here as greedily as the gulls on the nearby docks to get their fill of gorgeous Ashley River views while enjoying heaping omelets, eggs Benedict (served all day), and country-fried steak with sausage gravy. Service from the matriarchal staff is heartwarming and comes with near constant refills of coffee or sweet tea. Perhaps best known for breakfast, the restaurant also serves lunch and dinner. All menus are printed on well-used, blue-and-white laminate menus.

O'Hara & Flynn Wine and Cheese Shop, 225 Meeting St., downtown Charleston, SC 29401; (843) 534-1916; www.oharaand flynn.com; Wine Bar; $. The name sounds Irish, but this intimate space decidedly feels both "Euro" and neighborhood friendly. German-born owner Michael Franke greets all who enter his cozy domain with warmth, wit, and his extensive knowledge of wine. Bottle upon bottle are attractively stored on two walls of wooden bins stacked like tempting books in a highly drinkable library. An eclectic mix of tables, cushions, and comfortable chairs fills the center with full views of Meeting Street or of an antique wooden bar, depending on which way you're looking. Michael does exceptional pairings of wine or craft beer with assorted cheese he chooses himself with his very well-trained palate guiding the way. O'Hara & Flynn lilts with personality and charm and is the ideal place to stop and linger before or after dinner or for a restorative afternoon interlude.

Palmetto Cafe, 205 Meeting St. (at Charleston Place Hotel), downtown Charleston, SC 29401; (843) 722-4900; www.charleston place.com; American; $$$. Quiet and gorgeous in bamboo and plush banquette splendor, Palmetto Cafe begs to be a dining destination for sophisticated ladies-who-lunch or high-power business execs. Nestled neatly in the hushed confines of the Charleston Place Hotel (an Orient Express property), a soothing calm gurgles from a regal fountain in the lush courtyard garden the restaurant envelops.

Seats are deep and comfortable and the service is first class. The prices here are a bit steep (lunch options average between $15 and $20), but you get what you pay for. The towering seafood club is the ultimate composed sandwich stacked high with lobster, shrimp, bacon, smoked salmon, and tomato. A silky, pungent béarnaise for dipping brings it all together. Breakfast alternatives are similarly sophisticated and delicious and the Sunday brunch draws out locals and hotel residents alike for the omelet station and house-made caramel brioche.

Patat Spot Friet & Falafel, 41B George St., downtown Charleston, SC 29401; (843) 723-7438; www.patatspot.com; Dutch; $. It's hard to miss this relatively new hot spot on a trendy little street on the edge of the College of Charleston. If the bright fire-engine-red, sun-yellow, and sea-blue sign doesn't pull you in, the sinfully delicious herb-and-garlic aromas of freshly fried falafel and nutty Belgian friets will. The brainchild of bubbly co-owner and longtime food and beverage pro Phillis Kalisky Mair (she shares ownership with her husband Jeff), the restaurant pays homage to Holland, where she lived for many years. She dreamed of bringing a taste of Holland to Charleston, and Phillis and her staff do it spot-on right here. The falafel is fat and fried (or steamed if you prefer) fresh to order and packed with chickpea flavor. The "salad spot," a virtual mecca of Mediterranean specialties, is the place to top it off with more than

20 choices like baba ghanoush, plucky hummus, hot sambal sauce, zippy pickled red cabbage, and cooling yogurt and cucumber sauce. Don't forget the *friets!* They're hand cut, twice fried, and thick, and come stacked in imported cone holders. They, too, can be topped with a choice of more than 20 delicious sauces from a traditional, slightly sweet Dutch sauce (*patatje oorlog*), white-truffle oil and Parmesan, or try the cheese, salsa, and black-bean sauce. Ketchup's available too, but why not live dangerously and get your *friet* on the Dutch way?

Pearlz Oyster Bar, 153 E. Bay St., downtown Charleston, SC 29401; (843) 577-7251; www.pearlzoysterbar.com; Seafood/Oyster Bar; $$. Pearlz is a kind of old-world oyster bar with a hip, young twist—a true gem of a spot for slurping fresh and frigid oysters from their ice beds or warm from their steam bath. The refreshing mignonette sauce is full of clarity and flavor, but there is a zippy cocktail sauce at the ready for more traditional oyster-dressing fans. The menu doesn't stop there. Pearlz serves a gardenful of creative seafood and salad options and a buttery, chunky New England lobster roll as decadent as any you'd find on the rocky shores of Maine. The downtown location has a masculine feel and inviting booths and counters that are almost always occupied. Outside seating at bistro tables makes for excellent people-watching and eating on bustling East Bay Street. There is a newer Pearlz location in the happening area of Avondale in West Ashley, just minutes away, if you find yourself on the other side of the river (9 Magnolia Rd., West Ashley).

Pink Pig Bar & Q by Jim 'N Nick's, 288 King St., downtown Charleston, SC 29401; (843) 577-0406; www.jimnnicks.com; Barbecue; $. The faintest of breezes stirs 'cue-loving appetites and curls of fragrant smoke emanating from Jim 'N Nick's on this retail-rich stretch of King Street. The fact that this is a small but growing Birmingham, Alabama–based chain does nothing to dampen the deliciousness here. Pork is smoked for 14 long, tender, hours and is then hand-pulled and served with several plucky Jim 'N Nick–brand sauces. The succulent beef brisket may be the brightest star of all here, though, running neck and neck with the meaty, tender, smoked and slathered spareribs. Savor it with a side of carbs with the creamy, cheesy, crispy-topped mac 'n' cheese and piles of hot-from-the-oven, buttery cheese biscuits chased with an icy mug of brewed house ale. The homespun decor with touches of deco sophistication in the downtown setting is aesthetically perfect, but if you happen to be in North Charleston (about 20 minutes north of here) and have a hankering for some really good 'cue, there is a newer, second location there at 4964 Center Point Dr.

Social Restaurant + Wine Bar, 188 E. Bay St., downtown Charleston, SC 29401; (843) 577-5665; www.socialwinebar.com; Wine Bar/Restaurant; $$. A mostly late-night haunt for the young and beautiful since opening to rave reviews in 2007, Social is still pouring strong. With a selection of 400+ artisanal and sustainably produced wines and several choice craft beers hand-picked by wine-impassioned owner and Certified Sommelier Brad Ball, Social is a hot spot for oenophiles and foodies alike. Ball keeps things rolling and fresh from a 50-tap Cruvinet system at the bar, while Executive Chef Doug Svec heats up the kitchen with raw, self-taught talent. Whimsical "nibbles," and small plates of jasmine rice balls, wood-fired pizzas,  assorted sliders, and specialties like ginger-lacquered duck breast and saffron dumplings are served staggered, tapas-style, with the intention of being shared, which only adds to the Social social experience. Art by local artists rotate as regular embellishments to Social's black, nightclub-esque walls.

Thoroughbred Club, 205 Meeting St. (at Charleston Place Hotel), downtown Charleston, SC 29401; (843) 722-4900; www.charleston place.com; Tapas Bar/Tea/Bar; $$. Few things can top "a properly brewed pot of tea" and the accompanying pomp, circumstances, and crumpets that come with it. Splashed with deep red and brass, this little nook of a lounge off the spacious and magnificently appointed lobby of Charleston Place Hotel is just the right place to come inside, breathe deeply, and settle into a china cup or two of pure indulgence. Though the "club" serves tantalizing tapas in the afternoon and evening, and also has a fully equipped bar, tea stands out as the best reason to come. The tea selection is extensive and includes best-quality imported varieties as well as **Charleston Tea Plantation** (see p. 151) tea grown right here in Charleston. Femininity flutters from open-faced tea sandwiches, fresh baked scones, tarts, and crumpets served with whipped cream and lemon curd. You can even add some "bubbly" to the end of your afternoon tea experience. Tea is served from Thurs through Sun, 1 to 3 p.m.

Landmarks

Anson, 12 Anson St., downtown Charleston, SC 29401; (843) 577-0551; www.ansonrestaurant.com; Southern; $$$. Since opening in 1992, Anson's mantra has always been Lowcountry cooking, and more recently, Lowcountry cooking that follows seasonal and local inspiration. South Carolina–raised whole hogs are broken down in-

Puttin' on the Grits

Though Lowcountry chefs have been putting a gourmet spin on grits in recent years, whisking in cream and truffles and such, grits origins are humble. Once the breakfast fare of fishermen, grits mania has morphed into a veritable corn clamor! The best grits are wet stone ground and made from premium (preferably heirloom) corn varietals that once grew rampant throughout Charleston and the Lowcountry. The grinding gently separates the hull from the corn and breaks it down into grits, as well as cornmeal and polenta. Fortunately, local mills such as Anson Mills and **Geechie Boy Market and Mill** (see p. 145) are resurrecting milling traditions once almost lost to time and industrialization.

house to create Anson's celebrated fat pork chops, and whole corn is brought in to be ground in the restaurant's resident stone gristmill. This eventually becomes the pixie dust that coats everything from the melt-in-your-mouth cornmeal-fried okra, to the grits that form the pool for Anson's celestial interpretation of shrimp and grits prepared with Anson's house-cured bacon and roasted tomatoes. Expect fresh and local seafood across the board here and just see if you can resist the head-turning, signature crispy whole flounder brushed with an apricot-shallot glaze. Anson sits near the bustling

Old City Market, but has a refined sense of solitude and elegance, artfully set off by its sexy, wrought-iron French doors, smoky antique mirrors, and joyful cherubs. The European looks of the setting recall a distant locale like Paris or New Orleans, but Anson is decidedly and deliciously Lowcountry.

Carolina's Restaurant, 10 Exchange St., downtown Charleston, SC 29401; (843) 724-3800; www.carolinasrestaurant.com; Southern; $$$. Perhaps no restaurant says old-school Charleston as beautifully as Carolina's. Situated off a narrow, alleylike street just blocks from the water, its slightly off the beaten path location has been calling Charlestonians' names for decades. Its pale pink exterior is punctuated with a signature black awning and huge, arched windows. The popular bar invites with neighborhood charm, expertly mixed drinks, and the enduring appeal of the late, former chef Rose Durden's plump fried shrimp and crabmeat wontons. Much more than a friendly neighborhood bar, though, Carolina's also offers an upscale, casual dining room and the private, elegant seclusion of Perdita's Room. Executive Chef Jill Mathias is a Johnson & Wales grad with a talent and penchant for international influences, which she puts into play in dishes like calamari served with preserved lemon, sambal aioli, cilantro, mint, and basil and a succulent rib eye topped with the decadence of herbed marrow butter. Carolina's also offers complimentary valet parking.

Charleston Grill, 205 Meeting St., downtown Charleston, SC 29401; (843) 722-4900 or (888) 635-2350; www.charlestonplace.com;

Eclectic; $$$$. Dining at Charleston Grill feels a bit like taking an unforgettable vacation to an exotic locale. The expert staff, nightly, soothing live jazz music, exquisite food, fine wine (from a 1,300-strong list), and the grace and generosity of general manager and hospitality maestro Mickey Bakst permeate the entire space in such a way that you'll likely find yourself leaning back, sighing an audible sigh of relief, and settling comfortably into the night. Worries are not allowed here, only enjoyment. Executive Chef Michelle Weaver imbues the menu with minimalist inventiveness across four menu categories—Pure, Lush, Southern, and Cosmopolitan. In each, she "weaves" culinary magic in dishes like her perfectly airy, rich cauliflower soup with toasted truffle butter brioche croutons, butter-poached Maine lobster served with parsnips, preserved lemon and sweet corn puree, and the most divine, meaty, sweet crab cakes in all of Charleston, and perhaps on the entire planet. The enticing sway of the dining room is simultaneously relaxed and ethereal, which contrasts with the more earthy sophistication at the bar, where drinks are expertly mixed by some of Charleston's best bartenders. Warm salted nuts only add to the experience. Charleston Grill has received the Mobil Four-Star, AAA Four Diamond, and Distinguished Restaurant of North America Awards. Not surprisingly, it makes my Top Ten Must Do's list (see p. 17).

Circa 1886, 149 Wentworth St., downtown Charleston, SC 29401; (843) 853-7828; www.circa1886.com; American/Southern; $$$. Neatly tucked behind the towering heights of the elegant Wentworth Mansion, Circa 1886 is a one-of-a-kind restaurant in a one-of-a-kind setting. Housed in the original carriage house to the mansion (built in the year that Charleston endured a crippling earthquake), its romantic, arched booths, soft, sage-green colors, heart-of-pine floors, antique brick, and original wood-burning fire-places beg for a quiet dinner for two. Executive Chef Marc Collins, here since it opened in 2001, brands his menu with colonial-era influences that were unique to Charleston—particularly from the Caribbean, Europe, and Africa. The son of an artist, Collins' artistry and ingenuity are readily apparent in the beautifully crafted dishes, which are relatively light (compared to traditional Southern fare) and creatively seasoned with exotic spices. Begin any meal with Circa 1886's signature plantation rice bread rolls, then roll into chilled American lobster panna cotta with spiced pineapple relish and vanilla essence, or Carolina bass with toasted coconut, mango rum coulis, boniato bell pepper hash, and cilantro. Afterward, take a stroll around the historic cupola of the mansion next door for a birds-eye view of the old city. Circa 1886 holds both the Forbes Four-Star and the AAA Four Diamond ratings and has a 250-bottle wine list. The menu changes seasonally.

Cypress, 167 E. Bay St., downtown Charleston, SC 29401; (843) 727-0111; www.magnolias-blossom-cypress.com; Eclectic; $$$$. Another Top Ten Must-Do's list winner, Cypress is a restaurant that's finally getting the recognition it deserves under the leadership of James Beard–nominated Executive Chef Craig Deihl. He's been at the helm virtually since opening day in 2001 and has gradually taken Cypress and molded it into his own as he found and perfected his chef's "voice" here. Cypress mixes it up with Asian twists, such as the beef spring rolls with spiced cucumber and soy caramel and the crisp wasabi tuna, and plenty of Southern, especially in Deihl's exquisite, hand-crafted charcuterie. The charcuterie plate comes with a pungent, nutty house-made mustard, flaky biscuits, and house-pickled vegetables. The cosmopolitan, elegant setting, complete with a commanding 2-story wall of wine and views into a spacious, spotless kitchen, is custom-made for special-occasion dining, however Cypress's popular 3-course, $39 menu has broad appeal. Truly, who wouldn't love the exquisite chai-spiced panna cotta dessert with tangerine and candied ginger?

FIG, 232 Meeting St., downtown Charleston, SC 29401; (843) 805-5900; www.eatatfig.com; Eclectic; $$$. Longtime friends Chef-Partner Mike Lata and Manager-Partner Adam Nemirow bravely stepped out of the cocoon of secure food and beverage jobs (Lata was previously Executive Chef at **Anson,** see p. 40) to open their dream restaurant in 2003. FIG is an acronym for "food is good"; it should really be food is great! It's fresh and delicious at every turn. And FIG keeps getting better with more ambitious dishes like Lata's heavenly sheep's milk ricotta and mint gnocchi with Sea Island grass-fed beef Bolognese, while holding firmly to his sustainable and local-sourcing principles and classical French roots. The man has unparalleled skills maximizing the potential of the most humble ingredients from garden-fresh beets to Green Acre Farms eggs and transforming them, respectively, into purple orbs of impossible beauty and silky, homey deviled eggs. If there are better pureed potatoes than his buttery Yukon Gold version on this planet, I've yet to discover them. And FIG's signature chicken liver pâté may as well be *foie gras*—it's just that whisper-smooth and delicious. The restaurant world stood up and took notice in 2009 when Lata received the James Beard Best Chef Southeast Award, firmly planting him on the hallowed ground of one of the South's best chefs. FIG's long been one of my favorites, and thus makes it on the Top Ten Must-Do's List (p. 17). The mood here is relatively relaxed, with retro 1950s decor, and a comfortable bar at the front of the house. Still, dim lighting, professional service, and a 100-bottle wine list from small production winemakers (all under $100), make it a great spot for romantic dining, too. Don't forget to make reservations. FIG fills up fast.

Grill 225, Market Pavilion Hotel, 225 E. Bay St., downtown Charleston, SC 29401; (877) 440-2250; www.marketpavilion.com; Steak/Seafood; $$$$. Grill 225's mile-high, chocolate brushed-velvet banquettes, endless marble and mahogany, and 100% USDA Prime Quality Steak anchor the exclusive Market Pavilion Hotel at the corner of East Bay and South Market Streets in the heart of downtown. Some balk at the restaurant's lobby-central location, but there is no denying the lush beauty of the appointments or the quality of the beef or service here. Executive Chef Demetre Castanas takes great pride in his beef, which he insists be USDA Prime. He also insists on a minimum 42 days of wet aging for all cuts, but the fabled New York strips get a minimum of 50 days of aging love. Grill 225 shines with classic steak-house polish complete with ample chilled seafood platters, Maine lobsters (ranging from 3 to 5 pounds) served family style, and beef and chops served with assorted sides. The double-cut lamb chops, broiled colossal lump crab cakes served with tarragon cream and pineapple relish, creamed spinach, crunchy, buttery hash browns, and truffled potato chips with warm buttermilk blue cheese are all heady, intoxicating personal favorites. The white jackets and black bow tie–clad staff is formal, but this Greek, family-run affair of long-standing hoteliers and restaurateurs lends a real sense of warmth to the dining experience here. On warm evenings, head up to the Pavilion Bar on the top floor for beautiful views of the city and the harbor.

Husk, 76 Queen St., downtown Charleston, SC 29401; (843) 577-2500; www.huskrestaurant.com; Southern; $$$. A brand new restaurant baby at the time of this writing, Husk has already spun its way into the hearts of diners and critics near and far. It's an ultra-synthesized version of the direction in which Executive Chef Sean Brock has slowly been moving at the decidedly more formal **McCrady's** (see p. 50). At Husk, Brock drives home his impassioned Southern-only, seed-saving heirloom battle cry in a way no one else (at least in Charleston) has done before. The results are staggeringly delicious. Working in tandem with longtime kitchen partner, Chef de Cuisine Travis Grimes, the duo pickle and can their own veggies from Brock's garden, cure their own heirloom pigs, and insist on all things Southern (down to the olive oil and the salt) in their kitchen, which turns out a fresh menu daily that is dependent upon what their impeccably sourced farmers and purveyors deliver that day. There are a few things you can count on, though, whether you go for dinner (lunch) or supper (dinner). For example, Parker rolls that practically float they're so light and buttery, topped with sea salt and served in cloth sacks, Benton's bacon cornbread, and Husk chicken wings, which are brined, smoked, fried, and coated in a vinegary bath of pungent sweetness that will make you smile at the great-tastes gods. The setting, in a late 19th-century sprawling beauty of an old Charleston house, is bedecked with restrained Southern gentility in sweeping drapes that envelop the floor-to-ceiling original windows, gleaming glass, open hearths, and heart-of-pine floors. Next door is the most adorable kitchen house turned bar that you will ever see—brick and blood-red leather sofas made merrier with a muddled medley of Prohibition-era drinks and aged bourbon. Husk is on my Top Ten Must-Do's list (p. 17). Do it.

Magnolias, 185 E. Bay St., downtown Charleston, SC 29401; (843) 577-7771; www.magnolias-blossom-cypress.com; Southern; $$$. Like people, a lot of older, once ground-breaking restaurants are prone to resting on their laurels and dishing up mediocre versions left over from their glory days. Not so at Magnolias. In 1990, Donald Barickman rode into town with his expertly executed interpretations of "down South" cuisine at Magnolias, largely leading a restaurant renaissance (along with Frank Lee at **Slightly North of Broad,** see p. 53) that helped put Charleston on the national culinary radar. Many of today's chefs trained under Barickman (who recently retired), including current Magnolias Executive Chef Don Drake, who's been there since 1991. The food here is gutsy, utilizing a larder stocked with collards, tasso, country ham, and jasmine rice enhanced by classical training and finished with international brushstrokes in the kitchen. Favorite items that have been on the menu for years, such as the "Down South" egg rolls, rife with collards, chicken, and tasso served over a pepper puree with spicy mustard sauce and peach chutney, are fresh as a daisy and delicious as ever. Similarly, the luscious, round bends of wrought iron railings, huge magnolia-themed paintings, white linen tablecloths and able, professional service staff will never go out of fashion. Though it serves both lunch and dinner, Magnolias is an especially idyllic spot for an easy, lingering lunch.

McCrady's Restaurant, 2 Unity Alley, downtown Charleston, SC 29401; (843) 577-0025; www.mcradysrestaurant.com; Eclectic; $$$$. Listed as one of my Top Ten Must Do's (page 17), McCrady's is just that. It's stepped down a few notches of pretense and price in recent years while amping up a more unified culinary theme and infusing huge farm-to-table flavor under Executive Chef Sean Brock's guidance. Brock is *all* about authenticity, not just at the table, but in real life. This still humble man has received oodles of accolades recently, including the 2010 James Beard Best Chef Southeast award. Equal parts gastronome and farm boy, Brock is at ease practicing *sous vide* as he is pickling and canning the heirloom seed varietals on his own farm, or slaughtering his own heirloom pigs and forming them into one of the best charcuterie plates you'll find in town. The sophisticated bar in this circa-1788 Georgian former private home (and later tavern) is a comfy place to settle into choices from the regular menu or from the "bar snack" menu, posted on a blackboard and featuring homespun stuff like fried bologna with house-made mustard and duck rillettes on grilled baguettes. The dinner menu lists the farm and supplier source for everything, painstakingly selected by Brock. Scallops,

poached and seared with cauliflower, black garlic, and kumquat, are an excellent example of Brock's amazing ability to weave the humble with the sublime. Everything you eat here, including house-made rolls, will astound! The wine list, tended by Advanced Sommelier Clint Sloan, and the Prohibition-era mixed drinks aren't bad either.

Muse Restaurant & Wine Bar, 80 Society St., downtown Charleston, SC 29401; (843) 577-1102; www.charlestonmuse.com; Eclectic; $$$. Muse is a jewel-toned gem of a restaurant find situated on a quiet, almost exclusively residential street in the heart of downtown. Relatively new (having opened in 2007), Muse is the love child and brainchild of fourth-generation restaurateur Beth Anne Crane, who has a healthy fascination with Pompeii and the lost Villa of the Mysteries. The Villa is all but resurrected at Muse, which is awash in golden colors, throw pillows, frescoes, and an authentic Mediterranean patina rendering it both whimsical and wonderful. The cheerful-meets-romantic mood is perfectly embodied in the rambling rooms of the circa-1850 house that spills out onto candlelit open-air patios. Executive Chef Tom Egerton's fare embraces authentic flavors of the Old World with inspired, tasty twists. Orange, pomegranate, saffron, dates, and olives commingle with gorgeously fresh fish and pasta throughout the mesmerizing, nicely priced menu. Don't miss the seared Manchego cheese plate, which offers the creamy, melted nuttiness of the cheese, dotted with the peppery crunch of arugula and inviting salt of pistachios enveloped in a brilliant blood-orange vinaigrette. The whole fried Mediterranean sea bass is a worthy signature dish to put on the to-order list. More than 100 fine wines offered by the glass and over 500 by the bottle further enhance the Muse experience.

Oak Steakhouse, 17 Broad St., downtown Charleston; (843) 722-4220; www.oaksteakhouserestaurant.com; Steak House; $$$$. This graceful old dame looks over Broad Street like a sentinel, beckoning all in search of a great Certified Angus Beef Prime steak. Oak's soft, robin's-egg blue exterior is trimmed in white panels that frame towering windows enabling sweeping views of one of Charleston's most celebrated streets. Built in the 19th century, the elegant building still bears the lines of the bank building it once was, including a vault that is currently used to store and mature Oak's extensive wine collection. Executive Chef Jeremiah Bacon's precise, classical style and devotion to all things local and sustainable reflects his CIA (Hyde Park) training peppered with stints at famed, French-influenced kitchens, including Le Bernardin and Per Se. Bacon's Pittsburgh steak preparation affords a caramelized crunch of sugar that elevates the beefy, round, flavor of Prime meat to perfection, while his delicate soubise and gastriques seductively snake their way around beef and seafood dishes all over the menu. Dining here is an experience most heightened by a seat at one of the tables in the luscious and especially elegant top-floor dining room; bypass the often boisterous downstairs bar/ dining room if you're seeking the quiet, refined time that Oak offers best.

Peninsula Grill, 112 N. Market St., downtown Charleston, SC 29401; (843) 723-0700; www.peninsulagrill.com; Southern; $$$$.

Who would have thought Partner-Executive Chef Robert Carter's grandmother-inspired "Ultimate Coconut Cake" would come to dominate this formidable veteran chef's résumé? Yet with a whopping 12 layers of tender white cake and creamy coconut filling, it has, having garnered praise from all who enter its light and luscious world, including Bobby Flay who deemed it his "all-time favorite dessert." But this Southern gentleman's den has more to offer than just cake—it serves up Carter's gutsy yet refined Southern fare with a classic twist in sublime wild-mushroom grits with Lowcountry oyster stew, seared *foie gras* with duck barbecue, pepper biscuit, and peach jam, and beefy chops, steaks, and chilled seafood. Wash it all down with inventive cocktails, like a Bourbon Honey Old-Fashioned or a Southern Manhattan, in the soothing confines of the intimate, mahogany-lined bar that's always infused with the perfume of fresh flowers and the echoes of Charleston past. Nineteenth-century oil paintings of celebrated Charlestonians artfully stud the pale-gray velvet walls that surround a small sea of white linen and hushed elegance. An AAA Four Diamond restaurant, Peninsula Grill is one of Charleston's premiere dining destinations and has maintained that reputation since 1997.

Slightly North of Broad, 192 E. Bay St., downtown Charleston, SC 29401; (843) 723-3424; www.slightlynorthofbroad.net; Eclectic/ Southern; $$$. True to its name, this restaurant is located just a few blocks north of Broad Street, but it's better known by its acronym title—simply S.N.O.B. It's a tongue-in-cheek reference to the generalized notion that the people who live below Broad are snobs. For the record, they're not. It's about jocular good fun and deliciousness at S.N.O.B. Much of the feel-good energy can be credited to professional culinary veteran and South Carolina native, Executive Chef Frank Lee. Like **Magnolias'** Donald Barickman (see p. 49), Lee is another early-1990s ground-breaking chef who garnered attention with what was likely Charleston's first ever pad thai, and an almost manic dedication to sustainability and locally sourced purveyors well before it was considered cool. With his well-trained staff, Lee could easily lie back and take it easy, but he's a hands-on chef who's nearly always in the kitchen bobbing about in his signature red-pepper baseball cap. Lee's French classic-meets-Southern spin comes together swimmingly in dishes such as stuffed Carolina quail breast with cornbread tasso stuffing, buttermilk-fried leg, and sautéed spinach with a port-wine reduction, and grilled Maverick beef tenderloin, deviled crab cake and béarnaise and green-peppercorn sauce. Like Magnolias, S.N.O.B. serves both lunch and dinner, and is an especially popular lunch destination for local business and tourist crowds alike. Service is reliably professional and the setting feels like an elegant living room in an old Southern mansion, with ample banquettes, old mirrors, and a welcoming, antiqued patina.

Tristan, 10 Linguard St., downtown Charleston, SC 29401; (843) 534-2155; www.tristandining.com; Eclectic; $$$. A revolving door of chefs (all of them very talented), a series of menu and decor make-overs, and a challenging location amid the sometimes stifling herd of tourist traffic, have all led to a mild case of identity crisis at Tristan. As a result, it often gets overlooked and forgotten in the face of Charleston's formidable top restaurant contenders. That should not be the case. All of the changes and fine-tuning over the years have paid off and Tristan's star has never shined brighter. Executive Chef Nate Whiting provides a deft, cosmopolitan, and classical touch to Tristan's signature lamb ribs with hickory smoked, dark-chocolate barbeque sauce and added his own notes of balanced refinement in winners like a duck breast served with baked peach, brittle bread, and a *foie gras*–almond salad with a lavender-honey vinaigrette. The space is cool, airy, and quiet, cushioned with a nautical color scheme, a circle of deep, comfortable banquettes, and sheer drapes. A superb choice for a quiet, remarkable dinner, Tristan also serves a super-sophisticated and satisfying brunch on Sunday from 11 a.m. to 2:30 p.m. Live jazz music and bottomless Mimosas and Bloody Marys (for a $10 flat fee) go perfectly with Whiting's stellar Bergamo breakfast, which showcases a pool of melting Taleggio cheese topped with pudding-smooth polenta, soft-fried eggs, and an indulgent truffle–brown butter sauce. Take advantage of rare complimentary valet parking in the evening.

The Charleston Beer Exchange, 14 Exchange St., downtown Charleston, SC 29401; (843) 577-5446; www.charlestonbeer exchange.com; Craft Beer. Walking around Charleston's winding streets and alleys can build up a powerful thirst, especially in August. The Charleston Beer Exchange is the city's first and most comprehensive craft beer store. A revolving collection of rare lagers, ales, beer, and more are on tap from a changing series of growlers served from a super-knowledgeable and passionate staff. The storefront is small and inconspicuous on a cobblestoned side street, but it's not to be missed by beer aficionados. Rare Beer Tuesday is a popular night for tapping especially rare brews.

Christophe Artisan Chocolatier & Patissier, 363½ King St., downtown Charleston, SC 29401; (843) 297-8674; www.christophe chocolatier.com; Chocolates/Pastry; $$. The story behind Christophe is almost as sweet as third-generation chocolatier Christophe Paume's gorgeous, hand-painted chocolates. The Toulouse, France, native met his wife Carly when they were working for a chocolate company in Indiana, of all places. Both lovers of chocolate, they eventually fell in love with each other and got married. A smiling and gregarious Carly works the front of the house at the petite, *très Parisienne* boutique while pastry master Christophe works his chocolate wonders behind the scenes. The glossy, hand-painted beauties come in brilliant jewel tones and are truly, each and every one, a piece of art. Whether you go with the deep-chocolate goodness of the 72 percent cocoa hand-rolled truffles, the hand-painted cappuccino cheesecake chocolate, the Earl Grey tea dark chocolate hand-painted with a sky-blue coating, or any of the other myriad irresistible and unusual flavor pairings, you'll win. Paume also specializes in beautiful pastries and especially sinful éclairs. There is a second location at I'On in Mount Pleasant at 375 N. Shelmore Blvd., Unit 1B.

Heirloom Book Company, 123 King St., downtown Charleston, SC 29401; (843) 722-6377; www.heirloombookco.com; Book Shop. Talk about a cookbook lover's dream come true, and then some! Longtime cookbook collector and co-owner Brad Norton shares over 4,000 new, antiquarian, and collectible books from his personal collection. The books are neatly arranged, library style, in bright, white cubbyhole shelving. Chicken-wire lamps and soft, deep leather sofas invite lounging and reading in the sunny space, which is conveniently located on lower King, right across the street from the new **Bull Street Gourmet** (see p. 24), if reading about all that lovely food makes you hungry. In the back, there is a children's play space, complete with a pink, retro Easy Bake oven. Beyond that is a stunning orchid room full of beautiful plants lovingly tended by manager Carlye Dougherty. This area also serves as the Community Supported Agriculture basket pick-up place (thrice weekly). Heirloom Book Company, fittingly, also sells heirloom seeds and hosts regular book signings, wine and food tastings, and other locally oriented events.

The Olive Oil Shop, 316 King St., downtown Charleston, SC 29401; (843) 277-2707; www.theoliveoilshops.com; Olive Oil/ Vinegar Shop. Extra-virgin olive oil imported from all over the globe and balsamic vinegar (aged up to 18 years, in some cases) direct from Modena, Italy, infuse the air of this tiny shop with the huge, fruity flavors of the Mediterranean. The precious oil and vinegar are stored in Italian "fusties," which enable customers to pour and taste from the individual vats to find their favorites. Balsamic gets flavor infusions from exotic figs and pomegranates while olive oil gets pumped up with black truffles. Spices, stuffed olives, and gorgeous gift baskets are also available.

The Spice & Tea Exchange, 170A Church St., downtown Charleston, SC 29401; (843) 965-8300; www.spiceandtea.com; Spices/Tea; $–$$. Just one of a small and growing spice-shop chain based out of Saint Augustine, Florida, this fragrant, spice-lover's dream, gets a personal touch from proprietor Stacey Shea. She glides amongst the colorful pots of blends combined right in the shop (using customized recipes from the small corporate center), guiding curious customers with spot-on advice, often tested in her own kitchen, on how to best put the spices, salts, teas, and sugars to use. Shea's personal palate leans toward heat. Accordingly, she's a big fan of the Pirates' Bite, Thai Red Curry, and the Adobo Seasoning, which she puts in white chicken chili or anything that demands a special Latin American flavor. All who enter this shop are encouraged to open the large pots and smell away to their heart's content. She giggles when she tells the story of when Sean Brock of **McCrady's** (p. 50) entered the shop, and she proceeded (not knowing who he was) to give him a tutorial on the origins of paprika.

The Wine Shop of Charleston, 3 Lockwood Dr., downtown Charleston, SC 29401 (at the City Marina); (843) 577-3881; www .thewineshopofcharleston.com; Wine. Owner Debbie Marlowe has 3 decades of experience in wine, and practically bubbles with per-sonality and professional guidance at this small, well-stocked wine shop overlooking the City Marina and Ashley River. Marlowe's almost always on hand to help locals and tourists alike find the perfect gift or perfect wine pairing for that special dinner from a huge selection of wines ranging in price from a modest $10 or less a bottle to the more exclusive Collector's Wines. Friday night wine tastings with sunset views and 10% case discounts are as well-loved as Marlowe's welcome smile and generous spirit. The Marina Liquor store is next door for the harder stuff when the bar needs further stocking.

Learn to Cook

Charleston COOKS! 194 E. Bay St., downtown Charleston, SC 29401; (843) 722-1212; www.mavericksouthernkitchens.com; Cooking School/Shop. Equal parts kitchen retail shop and cooking school, Charleston COOKS! is a glittering vortex of culinary good-ness that teems with the energy and knowledge of the enthusiastic staff and tireless efforts of general manager and instructor, Danielle

Wecksler. Copper pans, Le Creuset Dutch ovens of every size, and spatulas in every color of the rainbow virtually beckon the curious cook to come inside, shop, and visit for a while. There is a vast collection of cookbooks and the store frequently hosts festive signings for local and nationally known visiting chefs. Next door is the sage-green kitchen and classroom that seems to endlessly emit enticing aromas from the many classes that are taught here on a daily basis, including the very popular Taste of the Lowcountry and Kitchen Fundamental classes. I've been on both sides of the counter as a visiting chef/instructor and class participant and I can't decide which is more fun. Both are always delicious!

Culinary Tours of Charleston, 40 N. Market St., downtown Charleston, SC 29401; (800) 918-0701; www.culinarytoursof charleston.com; Cooking Tours. Slip on comfortable walking shoes and pack an appetite for Charleston culinary knowledge and taste treats, and you're set to join Culinary Tours of Charleston. Centrally located in the heart of downtown, this small band of foodies leads faithful followers through the streets to visit restaurants, farmers' markets, bakeries, and more on the Savor the Flavors of Charleston Tour. Guests are rewarded with samples of Lowcountry favorites such as grits, pralines, sweet tea, and barbecue. The other tour, called simply The Kitchen Tour, is more of a celebration of Charleston chefs and restaurants and takes curious foodies on a tour of several prominent restaurants to visit their kitchens and meet their chefs. Both tours are walking tours, last 2½ hours, and provide a treasure trove of information and rare, inside peeks into places few outsiders have the opportunity to see.

Peninsular Charleston Above Calhoun Street

Twelve years ago, this section of town was all but dead in the food and restaurant department. **FISH** (p. 66) bravely set the trend and things kept rolling from there, even as the completion of the Arthur Ravenel Jr. Bridge in 2007 brought new highway exits and greater accessibility to the middle and upper levels of the peninsula. Encompassing a series of boroughs rife with quiet, intimate parks, schools, the medical district, lovely architecture, and relatively easy parking, the bulk of the in-demand restaurants are situated on King Street from Calhoun up to Columbus Street. But the parameters continue to expand with the growing demand for good eats in this delicious and varied restaurant and retail hot spot with a mildly bohemian mood.

Alluette's Cafe, 80 Reid St., peninsular Charleston, SC 29403; (843) 577-6926; www.alluettes.com; Southern/Soul; $$. Over the years, I've heard Alluette Jones, chef-owner of Alluette's Cafe, say countless times, "There is a reason the letters 'rest' are in restaurant." An adamant support of all things local (nearly all produce in the restaurant comes from local farmer Joseph Field), organic, and hormone/antibiotic-free, this Charleston-area native believes wholeheartedly in the power of food and attitude in healing body and mind. Alluette takes it slow in her pig-free kitchen (she wrinkles her nose in disdain at the mere mention of pork) to prepare her delectable "Geechi Girl" holistic soul food, and expects her guests in this cheerful, peach-colored cinderblock restaurant to do the same. Settle into the easy, languid mood here, especially on the sunny, outside porch area, while Alluette prepares the sweet, lightly battered and fried local shrimp with Geechi girl sauce, hand-cut organic fries, or the milky and mild shrimp salad for which she is justifiably revered.

Barsa, 58 Line St. (corner of King Street), downtown Charleston, SC 29403; (843) 577-5393; www.barsatapas.com; Tapas Bar; $$. Charleston's latest tapas spot is her best and also the one with

Gotta Getcha Geechee!

Gullah and Geechee (also spelled Geechi, as Alluette does) are names for a language and culture originally born in Africa. Gullah is believed to come from "Gola" and Geechee comes from "Kissi," which were both names of tribes living in and around Sierra Leone in West Africa, which is where many of the slaves that came through Charleston harbor and remained here in the rice-rich Lowcountry were from. The skills they learned growing rice in Africa helped fuel the wealth of rice plantation owners here. Because these slaves were resistant to malaria (which drove away many whites during peak season) and because many congregated in slave-exclusive communities (particularly in remote barrier islands), these slaves and their descendants preserved their language and many of their culinary and cultural traditions, from gumbo (a derivative of the African word for okra) to sweetgrass basket weaving, all of which are still practiced today.

the most authentic Spanish flair. Inspired by the street food and spirited sophistication of Barcelona, Barsa offers plenty of both. The robin's-egg blue exterior gives way to a cool, dark enclave of chocolate leather sofas and a soothing palette of black and gray, with the soft curves of retro antiques and Basque-style lantern lighting. At the center of it all is a commanding bar where drinks and small plates ebb and flow like sexy tango dancers. Sweet, fleshy, imported dates are filled with nutty Manchego cheese and wrapped with salty slivers of Serrano ham while gorgeous cubes of fried potatoes sizzle with fryer heat and made-to-order precision. The drunken-goat fondue is giddy with undercurrents of wine, goat cheese, and more nutty Manchego, made all the better with roasted vegetables and chewy bread for dipping. Barsa is a popular destination no matter what time of day or night, but is especially popular for Sunday brunch (and veggie-chunky, top-shelf Bloody Marys) and evening small-plate grazing.

Black Bean Co., 116 Spring St. (near Rutledge), peninsular Charleston, SC 29403; (843) 277-0990; www.blackbeanco.com; Vegan/Vegetarian; $. After all those sweet treats, let's take a guilt-free stop at this cheerful and healthful shop on Spring Street. Though not 100 percent vegan or 100 percent vegetarian (there are hefty sandwiches made with turkey, chicken, and cheese), this garden-fresh stop is mostly concerned with local, fresh produce and top-quality ingredients, nearly 80 percent of which come from local farmers at Thackery Farms, 100 percent of which has to be organic, and utensils and plates are 100 percent biodegradable. Cabbage and carrots crunch their way through spring rolls and salads, all dressed with inventive vinaigrettes and dressings (such as a fresh ginger marmalade) prepared by young and energetic Chef-Owner Ellis Grossman. The green mood and energy here (like the energy gyros and energy drinks) are youthful and, because of the freshness and clean, bright flavors of the food, you'll depart feeling satisfied yet light as air. Though small inside, the restaurant sustains a large pick-up, delivery, and catering business, which is conducted effortlessly through a state-of-the-art website, where ordering is as easy as pie. Most notable sandwich: the black and blue served with either chicken or turkey, blue cheese, a fig balsamic vinaigrette, black beans, and jasmine rice. A second location recently opened at 869 Folly Rd. on James Island; (843) 277-2101.

Closed for Business, 453 King St., downtown Charleston, SC 29403; (843) 853-8466; www.closed4business.com; Eclectic/Craft Beer Bar; $$. Owned by the same restaurant group (REV) as next door neighbor **Monza** (see p. 71) and **Taco Boy** (see p. 128), Closed for Business shares the group's impeccable conceptual clarity, in spite of its rather confusing name. CFB, as it's sometimes called, is indeed "open" for business with a combination of inviting pub fare such as an authentic Scotch egg served with pickled cabbage and Guinness mustard, a chunky braised duck potpie with earthy parsnips, leeks, and mushrooms, and the perfect pairing of a thick Tillamook cheddar and fontina grilled cheese sandwich with a steaming bowl of tomato soup. Soothing soul food at its best is prepared with locally produced vegetables and goods whenever possible and tastes even better consumed in this space, which features a fireplace and lounging area, comfortable, high-backed booths, and a long bar at the front of the house. The bar pours an ever-changing menu of fabulous local and imported light, white/ fruit, pale, amber/brown and dark ales, and beer draughts in 1-ounce, 16-ounce

and liter-size containers. You can even top your beer with a dash of sweet Lindeman's Framboise, if so desired.

Cupcake, 433 King St., downtown Charleston, SC 29403; (843) 858-8181; www.freshcupcakes.com; Cupcakes; $. If Cupcake's merry chocolate and pink stripes and fanciful flavors recall an old-fashioned ice cream shop, there is a reason. Owner Kristin Kuhlke Cobb finds her flavor inspiration while shopping the ice cream aisle at the grocery store. Rocky road, cookies and cream, and mint chocolate chip are three of the chunky, delicious "ice creams" turned cupcakes out of a total of 40 select flavors. Each of these is capped with Cupcake's signature, mile-high, curly-cue swirl of buttercream and select candies and sprinkles. The small, intimate shop cranks out 9 select flavors daily, including the silky smooth, Southern-inspired red velvet cupcake. I have a friend who cannot pass by without getting one (or two) on red velvet days. There is a newly opened shop at the Belle Hall Shopping Center at 644 Long Point Rd. in Mount Pleasant. The phone number there is (843) 856-7080.

FISH, 442 King St., downtown Charleston, SC 29403; (843) 722-3474; www.fishrestaurantcharleston.com; Eclectic; $$. FISH holds a couple of important firsts. It was one of the earliest restaurants to lead what would become a mad dash by restaurateurs and businesses to the Upper King Street district in 2000, and Nico Romo, FISH's executive chef and Lyon, France, native, is the youngest chef ever to earn the title of Master Chef of France. Bravo to this energetic, engaging chef who deftly combines Asian and French techniques and ingredients in his unique, refreshing seasonal and all-local menu. Fresh moo shu wraps take center stage during lunch hours, but Romo flexes his Gallic muscles with a tempting array of small and large plates during dinner. Sweet chili calamari takes an Asian dip in sesame tempura batter and curry crab soup gets a steam bun for Asian flair, but I like Romo's French stuff best, especially the whimsical chicken Cordon Bleu, which gets wrapped with pancetta and served with a bacon Emmentaler sauce or the rich, pork loin cassoulet. The decor is spacious and inviting with clean lines and flickering lights.

Five Loaves Cafe, 43 Cannon St., downtown Charleston, SC 29403; (843) 937-4305; www.fiveloavescafe.com; Soup/Sandwiches; $$. A pair of young, enthusiastic entrepreneurs infuse this super-charged soup and sandwich cafe with a mandate for freshness, free-range chicken, grass-fed, hormone-free beef, and a welcome mat for vegans and gluten-free eaters, to boot. All bread is made fresh daily in a local bakery, and succulent pasta comes from locally owned Bertolini Fresh Pasta Company. Sandwiches and salads are served half or whole and paired with an arsenal of delicious, seasonally inspired soups, if you so choose. Like everything here, best quality sandwich fillings are gourmet to a T, like peppercorn and horseradish rare roast beef (hormone-free, of course) with a pungent horseradish cream sauce or a piping-hot ham and

brie with green-tomato jam. The sunny, corner spot on Cannon leans toward bohemian and cheerful in mood, with interesting little quips and quotes from noted personalities pasted to the light-blue booths and assorted tables. The cafe becomes more of a restaurant at night with a broad menu of more substantive entrees and wine selections. Five Loaves Cafe has a second location over the Arthur Ravenel, Jr. Bridge in Mount Pleasant at 1055 Johnnie Dodds Blvd., Ste. 50; (843) 849-1043.

La Fourchette, 432 King St., downtown Charleston, SC 29403; (843) 722-6261; www.lafourchettecharleston.com; French; $$$. La Fourchette is so endearingly French and delicious, Francophiles from near and far flock to this diminutive bistro to say *oui* (and *oui* and *oui*) to Brittany-born Perig Goulet's authentic bistro fare while soaking up his infectious energy, generously seasoned with a very strong and very proud French accent. Ancient brick walls, small bistro tables, and rustic decor make it decidedly easy to settle into a romantic evening at a surprisingly easy price. Goulet keeps the menu abbreviated, but 100 percent French. The double-fried *pommes frites* are cooked in duck fat and the homemade duck pâté is so closely tied to his French roots, Goulet refuses to share the recipe, instead encouraging you to "just eat it, eh?" Imported cornichons, French Dijon mustard and crisp croutons make it impossible not to do just that, with a smile, to boot. All of the 60 or so bottles of wines at La Fourchette are French and hand-picked by Goulet, a long-standing restaurant and food-and-beverage professional who first learned to cook in his mother's kitchen, *bien sûr*.

Macaroon Boutique, 48 John St., downtown Charleston, SC 29403; (843) 577-5441; www.macaroonboutique.com; Bakery/ French; $. Yet another sweet surprise, this one is utterly French and beguiling, beginning with pastry chef/owner Fabrice Rizzo's lilting French purring from the bustling, back-room kitchen and ending with a single bite of one of his expertly crafted *macarons*—especially the pistachio or raspberry variety. It's ooh-la-la, love at first bite and it just keeps growing deeper with the *pithiviers,* croissants, seasonal fruit and savory turnovers, and (beware!) the addictive salty/sweet chocolate cookies. A French native with a decorated résumé, Rizzo is the consummate perfectionist and his passion and love for his craft is palpable and irresistible. His doll-like and adorable wife, Fabienne, is often found at the front of the store, neatly and lovingly packing this food *bijoux* in adorable little boxes that scream Paris. Macaroon will make anyone swoon, and that's why it's on my Top Ten Must-Do's (see p. 17). Pick up an oven-fresh, crusty baguette and a neat packet of ribbon-wrapped macaroons after the nearby **Charleston Farmers' Market** (see p. 85) and your day of deliciousness is about to begin. An additional location/kitchen recently opened at 334 E. Bay St., downtown Charleston. Here, parking is easier, but I'm particularly attached to the European, boutique-feel of the original shop. *Bon appétit!*

Martha Lou's Kitchen, 1068 Morrison Dr., peninsular Charleston, SC 29403; (843) 577-9583; Southern/Soul; $. Baby blue and pink all over, Martha Lou's Kitchen's eye-catching color scheme stands out from the gray dinginess of the rather industrial stretch of Morrison Drive upon which it sits. Inside, Chef Martha Lou Gadsden's warm and tiny kitchen hums with heart and decades of practiced home-style soul cooking by the round, soft, and petite dame herself. Along with the assistance of her daughter Debra, Gadsden cranks out made-to-order fried chicken, pork chops, fried whiting, and stews lima beans from a clanking battery of battered, cheap pots seasoned with love. The dirty rice, round and buttery spicy/sweet okra soup, and the best fried chicken you can ever hope to eat, are served on Styrofoam plates with plastic utensils, but that doesn't diminish the experi-

ence. The tables are lined with cheerful floral and gingham linens and the service is so friendly and charming that coming here feels like coming home every time. The meat 'n' three menu revolves daily, but thank goodness the fried chicken, the main reason Martha Lou's Kitchen makes my Top Ten Must Do's list (see p. 17), is served every day.

Moe's Crosstown Tavern, 714 Rutledge Ave., peninsular Charleston, SC 29403; (843) 722-EATS; www.moestaverns.com; Burgers; $. Burgers at this long-favorite watering hole come extra fat and juicy and gussied up with gourmet surprises such as goat cheese and roasted poblano peppers that somehow seem out of place in this slightly sticky, dark bar/restaurant on the edge of Hampton Park. The restaurant recently underwent renovations, but the gooey grub remains a smashing fit with free-flowing tap and bottled beers and sports-intensive programming on multiple television sets. By day, Moe's draws an eclectic blend of bow-tied businessmen and college kids; by night it seems like the whole town turns out for Moe's almost world-famous hand-cut fries, especially on half-price burger night (Tuesday). Poland comes to town in dishes like Papa T's pierogies and Polish kielbasa served on a thick hoagie roll with Polish mustard, both reflecting the owner's Polish heritage. There is a second, not quite as timeworn location further downtown at Moe's Downtown Tavern, 5 Cumberland St.; (843) 577-8500.

Monza, 451 King St., downtown Charleston, SC 29403; (843) 720-8787; www.monzapizza.com; Pizza; $$. Just walking down the street is enough to get any Neapolitan pizza fan revved up for Monza's magic. Stoked by a 1,000 degree F, wood-fired oven that infuses the air with pizza perfume, each pie is prepared to order with wheat flour, yeast, and water all imported from Italy and most are finished with milky-smooth *fior di latte* mozzarella. Monza's named after the legendary racetrack in Italy and makes it to the finish line with style every time with pizzas named after Italian race greats like Volpini and Count Louis, topped with the freshest, local ingredients, and washed down with cool Italian beer and wines. Don't stop at the pizza, though. The butterbean salad, tossed with olive oil and lemon and topped off with local, Lowcountry shrimp, tastes as sweet as the summer, and sausage and pepper sauce with moist, ricotta meatballs are magnificent. The decor is as sexy and sleek as a Ferrari and so is the crowd.

O-Ku, 463 King St., downtown Charleston, SC 29403; (843) 737-0112; www.O-Kusushi.com; Sushi/Japanese; $$$. O-Ku, with its winning sushi, delicious dim sum, and superbly executed Japanese specialty dishes from miso marinated Chilean sea bass to lobster *yaki udon*, proves it's more than OK. Arguably the best sushi in what's a relatively sushi-starved town, O-Ku adds a stellar setting to the mix, a setting that's both cosmopolitan and minimalist, but warmed with antique brick walls and oversized retro, 1950s-esque lighting. Executive Chef Sean Park, a native of Seoul, South Korea, sharpened his Japanese culinary chops under Sekigami Chiro in New York and rolls sushi like a master. You can usually spot him in his chef's whites over long shorts and clogs working the open kitchen, smiling away. The chic and beautiful come to O-Ku in droves to soak up the "see and be seen," sleek atmosphere for the after-work and late-night bar scene that features amazing specialty cocktails—the best is the refreshing ginger basil lemonade prepared with a fresh ginger syrup and a veritable garden of freshly muddled basil. For a quieter experience, and one that affords open views of the beautifully appointed dining room, come earlier (before 6 p.m.) for dinner or for O-Ku's popular and delicious bento box (and more) weekday lunch service. Don't leave without sampling the crunchy, hot tempura rock shrimp lightly tossed in fresh, spicy aioli over fresh greens that's served from the dinner menu.

181 Palmer, Culinary Institute of Charleston/Trident Technical College—Palmer Campus, 66 Columbus St., peninsular Charleston, SC 29403; (843) 820-5087; www.culinaryinstituteofcharleston .com; Cooking School/Cafe; $$. Want to eat like a millionaire on a student's budget? Make 181 Palmer at the **Culinary Institute of Charleston/Trident Technical College** (see p. 87) your destination, pronto! Tables are lined with white linens and sparkling glass in this pristine, bright space, located adjacent to the culinary school's cooking lab where students, under the guidance of chef/mentor Scott Stefanelli, create world-class fare at cafeteria (well, almost) prices. The room radiates with young, positive energy, as student servers cheerfully deliver dishes created by their fellow classmates in the nearby glassed-in kitchen. A new seasonal menu is created every semester, designed to challenge and expand students' skill sets with impressive dishes like puree of roasted cauliflower soup with golden raisins and brown-butter emulsion, ricotta gnocchi with local pork Bolognese, and maple pots de crème with blood-orange marmalade and sugar and spice brioche doughnuts. Three delicious courses—an appetizer, entree and dessert—ring in for a meager $15. One small catch, reservations are required and the student restaurant closes briefly between semesters. Visit the website for menu, hours, and to make reservations. Reservations can also be made by telephone.

Pane e Vino, 17 Warren St., downtown Charleston, SC 29403; (843) 853-5955; www.panevinocharleston.com; Italian; $$. Tucked away down a smaller street off of bustling King Street, Pane e Vino affords a soothing, romantic, and infinitely Italian journey into culinary and oenophile delight without even having to set foot on a plane. A spacious outside patio is anchored with a massive live oak tree and swaying lanterns. Pane e Vino has taken on an inviting patina over the decade it's been around and has renewed vitality under the recent ownership of Northern Italy native Alfredo Temelini. He takes cues from his grandmothers' Emilia-Romagna kitchens as well, weaving wonders in dish after dish. Ultrathin sliced shiitake mushrooms are deep fried and blessed with sea salt and truffled Pecorino cheese while homemade spinach and ricotta ravioli melt into a prosciutto and asparagus pool of creamy sauce. Save room for added substance in the long, slow braised, fragrant lamb shank served over soft polenta with a rich, demi-glace prepared from a pan-sauce reduction. On cooler nights, the small, inside dining room, cloaked with dark wood and dim lights, feels as inviting as grandmother's kitchen. You can almost feel the warmth of maternal love here and you can especially taste it in the fresh baked daily bread. The wine list is moderately varied and priced and is composed entirely of Italian regional wines.

Paolo's Gelato Italiano, 41 John St., downtown Charleston, SC 29403; (843) 577-0099; Gelato; $. The Euro flags fly high at this cool Italian gelato store, situated squarely between **39 Rue de Jean** (see p. 82) and **Macaroon Boutique** (see p. 69). When

Paolo, a tall, lanky, raven-haired Roman god of a guy (complete with a bouncy Italian accent) is there, the tiny, Italian candy–kissed space sparkles particularly brightly. Flavors rotate daily from a total of 75 gelatos, and include a pale green, nutty pistachio and a stellar mascarpone and balsamic gelato blend. Crunchy waffle cones and sprinkles make eating gelato especially fun. Paolo's is a great place to cool off on a hot day or top off a meal on a sultry summer evening. Settle down outside on a nearby bench and soak up the European romantic touch in this part of town. No seating is provided inside. Remember to bring cash, though. Paolo's is cash only and pricier than a quick stop at DQ.

Santi's Restaurante Mexicano, 1302 Meeting St. Rd., peninsular Charleston; (843) 722-2633; Mexican; $$. Per his edict, everything is made and prepped by hand at Santi's under the patient tutelage of co-owner and Mexican native Santiago Zavalza. Whole chickens simmer with garlic, and strategic seasonings fill enchiladas, small Mexican tacos, quesadillas, and more with huge, mellow flavor. Dishes are often topped with cilantro and lime or, if you pick super wisely, Santi's show-stopping, dark-brown, spicy mole sauce. A basket of freshly fried, warm flour tortilla chips and a cruet of fresh tomato salsa start every meal, gratis. Locals know to order the house's special Mexican soup prepared with what seems like ladles of the poached chicken infused with fresh lime juice and grandmother's kitchen goodness. Super-easy parking in a spacious, mostly dirt-lined lot is almost always full at both lunch and dinner. Outside dining is especially enjoyable on a pretty day and people-watching is always interesting here. I'm particularly intrigued by the loyalty of the local Coast Guard who fill the place with a sea of blue uniforms on any given day. A second location recently opened at 114 Holiday Dr. in Summerville; (843) 722-2633.

Sugar Bakeshop, 59½ Cannon St., downtown Charleston, SC 29403; (843) 579-2891; www.sugarbake.com; Bakery; $. Baby blue, pure white, and pristine, Sugar is spun from pure love. Owners Bill Bowick and David Bouffard ditched NYC for Charleston to make their Sugar dream come true, and what a sweet dream it is. Tarts, cookies, cupcakes, cakes, and more are made daily and artfully arranged in the retro glass counters as a small team of bakers stay busy taking care of you. The seasonally inspired cupcakes are especially inspirational in late winter months when fresh citrus is in ample supply. Zest and juice of fresh lime infuse the coconut lime cupcakes with lip-smacking joy, even as the vibrant orange buttercream naps the moist, real vanilla cupcakes. Thursday is Lady Baltimore cupcake day, which celebrates the famous cake with the grace of sherry-infused figs and raisins all topped off with a light-as-air meringue. Sip some of Sugar's mint and honey house-made sweet tea in the inviting open-air garden while nibbling on the crunchy, buttery, and hot/sweet ginger molasses cookie. Caramel cupcakes (or cake) are swaddled in the most heavenly caramel buttercream icing that will make you want it to be Wednesday, caramel cake day, every day.

Virginia's on King, 412 King St., downtown Charleston, SC 29403; (843) 733-5800; www.virginiasonking.com; Southern; $$. A lifetime of cooking for her familial brood helps bring Charleston-native Virginia Bennett's refined, family-style Southern cooking to the table at Virginia's. Trickle-down cooking and meal memories from the Sunday (and later Thursday) family dinners she served for her large family taste smashing for breakfast, dinner (lunch) or supper (dinner). I know the names can get confusing, y'all, but there is nothing confusing about the actual food. The recipes are from Virginia's home recipe box and get expert treatment in the kitchen here to produce crisp-from-the-fryer, batter-dipped fried okra served, heaping, on thick, white country plates with decadent pools of smoked, peppery, house-made aioli. Pulled-pork sliders come on flaky sweet potato biscuits, and thick slabs of moist meatloaf come slathered with dark, caramel-colored pan gravy. A host of sides from baked macaroni and cheese to eggy, breaded sweet squash casserole taste extra delicious in the slightly sophisticated setting which balances gentility with antiquity surrounded by old brick walls, honey-hued wood tables, and friendly service. Benedicts made with real hollandaise and the fried green tomato BLT served on fat Texas toast make their mark at breakfast with sparkling mimosa libations that would certainly make Virginia proud.

WildFlour Pastry, 73 Spring St., peninsular Charleston, SC 29403; (843) 327-2621; www.wildflourpastry.com; Bakery; $. Sundays at WildFlour Pastry offer a new kind of church to the faithful worshippers of an edible God of a different kind—fresh-from-the-oven, yeasty, fluffy sticky buns slathered with gooey white icing or a shower of toasted pecans. From 8 a.m. to 1 p.m. on Sunday, the bun people arrive to line up around this button of a shop, patiently awaiting the blessed offering served amid the din of whirring steamed milk and neighborly banter. Smack in the middle of it all, always, is hands-on Chef-Owner Lauren Mitterer, issuing warm smiles and bear hugs to all who will receive. The CIA grad (Hyde Park, New York) and multi-award-winning pastry chef remains true to her maternal homespun fare throughout the work week at WildFlour, assembling, from scratch, the likes of fat double-chocolate cookies, custards, crumbly, buttery coffee cakes, and a barista-like arsenal of specialty teas and coffees. Mitterer also has a passionate knack for assembling beautiful, original specialty cakes for any occasion from weddings to birthdays.

Basil, 460 King St., downtown Charleston, SC 29403; (843) 724-3490; www.basilthairestaurant.com; Thai; $$. Consistency, precision and pure Thai talent quickly established Basil as Charleston's Thai King nearly a decade ago when it opened, a throne Basil still proudly and deservedly holds to this day. At the center of the maelstrom in the tiny, easily viewed open kitchen reigns Thailand-native chef Suntorn Cherdchoongarm (say that five times fast!) coolly overseeing the made-to-order creation of Basil's signature curries, stir fries, noodles, spring rolls, and cool, crisp salads. His formula for success includes a fully prepped *mise-en-place* and carefully balanced and prearranged, freshest-only ingredient trays, ensuring that everything tastes reliably the same and exquisitely delicious with each visit. His special blend sauces are the crowning glory, especially in signature dishes like the crispy red curry duck and squeaky-fresh basil rolls. The sunny colors and bright flavors of the *tom ka gai* (chicken coconut soup) would bring a smile to the saddest day; it's one of my favorite things here and can be ordered either in a cup or a bowl. Look for a green neon light with an antique bike on top, Basil's hallmark beacon in the heart of Upper King Street restaurant row. Basil's always packed, but service is quick, in the animated, sometimes noisy space. There is quieter outside seating available, good weather willing. Basil offers a diverse and well-balanced wine list, served by the glass or the bottle, to pair with the piquant fare.

Halls Chophouse, 434 King St., downtown Charleston, SC 29403; (843) 727-0090; www.hallschophouse.com; Steak/Seafood; $$$$. If it weren't for the fact that the prime, dry-aged beef at this AAA Four Diamond restaurant is so succulent and delicious and the original art and design of the dining rooms so appealing, I probably wouldn't have included Halls in this book at all. Service at this family-run business is often clumsy and sophomoric. And there is something distasteful about the repetitive, cloying greetings-turned-space-invading-assaults from the staff and  owners. Plus, Halls is painfully pricey, with steaks averaging $50 and the prime porterhouse topping it off at a whopping $68. (And that's all a la carte.) That said, the steaks are probably the best in town, and steak-house favorite sides like creamed spinach and onion rings are top-notch. Executive Chef Matthew Neissner is a talented chef who, in addition to the steaks, really knows how to make the accompanying sauces shine. Halls goes out of its way to satisfy vegans, vegetarians, and children, too.

Hominy Grill, 207 Rutledge Ave., downtown Charleston, SC 29403; (843) 937-0930; www.hominygrill.com; Southern; $$. Look for the pink house with a giant mural of a pretty waitress holding a bowl of butter-topped, steaming grits or the usual crowd of hungry fans that gather greedily outside, awaiting any one of Chef-Owner Robert Stehling's plates of Southern goodness, and you'll know you've arrived at Hominy. Be glad you did! This is some of the very best food you can get in Charleston. Mile-high, flaky biscuits, buttermilk pie, cornbread, fried chicken, vegetable plates (including succulent, sweet squash casserole and stewed tomatoes, if you choose), local-only fresh fish, bacon and scallion enriched shrimp and grits, deep, dark and delicious chocolate pudding; whatever your pick for breakfast, lunch, dinner, or weekend brunch, you simply cannot lose. This 2008 James Beard Best Chef Southeast winner learned how to cook at the celebrated Crook's Corner in Chapel Hill, followed that with a stint in some kitchens in New York City, and came home to roost in Charleston at Hominy, his very own baby. Despite the accolades, Stehling tends his baby in hands-on fashion. The humble chef is almost always in his tiny kitchen wearing his signature bandanna, making sure everything's getting done just right. The setting is homey and casual. Because Hominy's so very popular and relatively small, it can be loud at peak hours. It's a small price to pay, believe me. On weekends, go early or go late to avoid a long line. Any time of day, Hominy Grill is always on my Top Ten Must Do's list (see p. 17). See Hominy Grill's recipe for **Cheese Grits** on p. 217.

Lana Restaurant & Bar, 210 Rutledge Ave., downtown Charleston, SC 29403; (843) 720-8899; www.lanarestaurant.com; Mediterranean; $$$. Situated kitty-corner and across the street from Hominy Grill on this griddle-hot restaurant corner, Lana is light years away in terms of culinary style, but equally gutsy and delicious as Hominy, in its own sun-kissed, Mediterranean way. The food is Southern—Southern European, that is. Executive Chef John Ondo visits various regions of Spain, Italy, Morocco, France, and more in tongue-tingling dishes from an invigorating *salade niçoise* to mussels in a spicy tomato broth with pancetta, roasted garlic, parsley, and white wine. The food here always dances with fresh, bright flavors. The mood is elegant, with red booths, dark wood, and dim lighting, and the dining here is always welcoming and completely without pretense. Co-owner and Bosnia native Drazen Romic is a giant of a man at 6 feet, 6 inches tall, and his warmth and professionalism infuse the diminutive dining room, even as Ondo's handsome red head bobs busily through the small window into the kitchen. Prices are comparatively gentle considering the high quality of the delicious ingredients, and the gently priced wine list is diverse and international, just like the menu. Serving both lunch and dinner, Lana provides an instant European getaway for a romantic evening or fun with friends, without the aggravation or expense.

39 Rue de Jean, 39 Jean St., downtown Charleston, SC 29403; (843) 722-8881; www.39ruedejean.com, French; $$$. Who would have thought this *très Parisienne* brasserie would have built the bulk of its very good reputation on big, beefy burgers and smashing sushi, especially since neither one is particularly pervasive in Paris? Yet that's exactly what this enigmatic culinary charmer managed to do since it opened nearly 15 years ago. At first most hotly pursued for a seat at its then trendy and hot bar for 20- and 30-somethings, it quickly garnered praise for the hot stuff coming out of the kitchen, including killer bistro requisites like onion soup gratinée, escargots, *frites* and *moules*. All the while, "Rue," as she's affectionately known, has stayed on the good-food track, and like a fine wine, gotten even better with time. These days the kitchen is in the ultra-capable hands of Executive Chef Aaron Lemieux, a man who has his way with quiche, transforming it into a virtual soufflé—an airy custard concoction encased in a flaky, house-made pastry and filled with whatever his daily muse inspires. Huge, antiqued mirrors dominate over the large, masculine space while flirty servers in ruffled white aprons and simple black dresses soften the edges. Lunch, dinner, or weekend brunch, you can always count on the Rue. There is a complete and varied wine list of French and international varietals to wet your whistle.

Trattoria Lucca, 41-A Bogard St., peninsular Charleston, SC 29403; (843) 937-3323; www.luccacharleston.com; Italian; $$$. Ken Vedrinski, the chef-owner of this wholly authentic and delightful Italian trattoria, will be the first to tell you he loves Italian food. But he doesn't have to. One bite, and you can taste it. Vedrinski, a highly decorated chef with a list of awards too long for this space, including multiple James Beard nominations, first learned to cook from his Italian grandmother and he hasn't stopped since. At Lucca, the source of inspiration comes from the ancient Tuscan city of the same name, the home of some of the world's finest olive oils. You'll find them here, in this purple and cream–pillowed, plush nook, along with imported charcuterie, cheese, and more of the highest Italian order. Vedrinski combines them with a blend of raw passion and well-honed talent, mixing in a larder of farm-to-table produce and local fish to create food miracles. His handmade pastas drip with goodness and are deftly sauced in unforgettable dishes such as the *bucatini* with a San Marzano tomato *sugo, polpette,* and Ragusano cheese. The golden beets dressed with white balsamic vinegar, pickled garlic, tangerine, chile flakes, and walnuts is pure flavor divinity. On Monday night, Lucca hosts a very popular and heartwarming Family Style Supper that offers four courses (less than $40) from the menu, served communal-style. A few doors down, Vedrinski's 100 percent Italian wine, beer, cheese, and charcuterie shop, Enoteca, begs for a pre-dinner antipasto stop or a late-night nosh and sip. Enoteca is located at 18 Percy St.; (843) 577-0028.

Specialty Stores, Shops, Markets & Producers

Charleston Bloody Mary Mix, (843) 737-0651; www.charleston mix.com; Cocktail Mix. A fruitless late night search for a decent Bloody Mary mix inspired friends Ryan Roberts and Ryan Eleuteri to create their own blend. Drawing on their mutual restaurant experience and Southern roots, they sought to create "The Bloody Mary, Perfected." Indeed, by all accounts they have! The spicy tomato blend uses local ingredients only and is brewed and bottled right here in Charleston. The mix combines several ingredients close to Charleston's culinary heart and history, including the flavor key, rice vinegar. Worcestershire sauce (imported from England), sea salt, ground peppercorns, fresh tarragon, thyme,

and a splash of fresh orange juice seal the flavorful deal. The plucky beverage is served all around town at various restaurants (just ask for it!) and a long and growing list of retailers in Charleston and Hilton Head, South Carolina. The mix can be purchased directly from the website (see address above), but is limited to a maximum of 12 bottles, or a case. See Ryan Roberts' and Ryan Eleuteri's recipe for **Hot Pickled Okra Bloody Marys** on p. 218.

The Charleston Farmers' Market, Marion Square, between King and Meeting Streets, downtown Charleston, SC 29403; Farmers' Market; $. April kicks off the seasonal fun at the always festive Charleston Farmers' Market; fun and flavor that will last as long as Charleston's long growing season, which wraps up just before Christmas. Every Saturday from 8 a.m. to 2 p.m., the area's best farmers congregate with what seems like the entire community flocking under a sea of white canopies to stock their larders with freshly picked gems of the season, artisanal meats and cheeses, seafood, bread, pickles, flowers, and more. Twice named by *Travel + Leisure* as one of the best farmers' markets in the US, it's one of my Top Ten Must Do's in Charleston (see p. 17) and a great place to shop for a picnic on the square when the shopping's done. Some of the best bets for really, really good eats include: The Pickle Lady (Alexis Dewil); Charleston Crepe Company, for an outrageous sweet and/or savory crepe; Roti Rolls organic sandwiches; Thackery Farms' always gorgeous produce stand for a passel of garden crunch; Bertolini Fresh Pasta Company; and Houser Meats' cured, artisanal meats and best-ever bacon. Keep your eyes peeled for local chefs doing their shopping while you're there. Cash is best for produce and smaller purchases, but credit cards are also acceptable in some cases.

Palmetto Brewing Company, 289 Huger St., peninsular Charleston, SC 29403; (843) 937-0903; www.palmettobrewingco .com; Craft Beers. Entrepreneurs Louis Bruce and Ed Falkenstein joined forces in 1994 to open Charleston's very first brewery since the Prohibition era and create what they deem "Charleston's Original Beer." The duo produce four delicious, hand-crafted brews with distinct flavors and broad appeal: The best-selling "Amber," Pale Ale, Charleston Lager, and the dark, rich, roasted malt–infused Porter. The brews enjoy broad distribution around greater Charleston and in Hilton Head, South Carolina.

3.14 Pies, 654 King St., downtown Charleston, SC 29403; (843) 608-8314; www.314piescharleston.com; Pies. Owners Brent and Lindsay Doolittle made their pie-in-the-sky dreams come true when they opened their own artisanal pie factory downtown. The duo traveled and tasted pies the world over to come up with their delicious pie themes that emphasize artisanal method, organic and seasonal ingredients, and truly fun interpretations of old classics like Joyful Almond Pie (a riff on the classic Almond Joy candy bar) and the festive Pistachio Orange Blossom Pie. Select from the "Downtown" or "Downhome" collection by the pie or by the slice from seasonally changing menus. Whole pies can be delivered to your doorstep with an advance order, picked up at the shop by appointment, or are available by the slice at a growing number of local restaurants and retailers, including **Caviar & Bananas** (see p. 26).

Learn to Cook

Culinary Institute of Charleston/Trident Technical College, Two campuses: Palmer Campus, 66 Columbus St., downtown Charleston, SC 29403 and Main Campus, 7000 Rivers Ave., Building 920, North Charleston, 29406; (843) 574-6152 (registration); www .tridenttech.edu/1453.htm; Cooking School. Interested in boning up on your culinary acumen while in Charleston? Both campuses of this local culinary training powerhouse offer a host of continuing education classes to the general public. From "A Toast to Hospitality" to "Dinner Party Planning," these classes offer a fun, educational, and affordable menu of cooking classes. The class options change with each semester and fill quickly, so call ahead or check in at the website to select and reserve a seat.

North Charleston, Hanahan, Goose Creek, Moncks Corner, Summerville

These towns, situated above the peninsula, stack upon each other like so many unique dominoes stretching north, until finally reaching Summerville, approximately 30 miles north of downtown. Each has a distinct personality, ranging from the bucolic at the lovely **Mepkin Abbey** (see p. 101) in Goose Creek, to widespread suburbia (and occasional shady sections) in North Charleston. Summerville, also called Flowertown, is a fragrant haven of towering pine trees year-round and showcases wide swaths of jewel-toned azaleas in the spring. Its historic district boasts a string of languid, broad-porched bungalows and vast estates that wind through the heart of the town. The charming, pedestrian-only block of Central Avenue is where you'll find neighborhood favorites **The Eclectic Chef** (see p. 90) and **The Perfect Wife** (see p. 94). Each of these towns possesses compelling culinary reasons to visit, especially if you're in this neck of the woods. Bring your car keys, though, it's a long walk from downtown. Enjoy the ride!

Foodie Faves

Aunt Bea's Restaurant, 1050 E. Montague Ave., Park Circle in North Charleston, SC 29405; (843) 554-3007; www.auntbeasrestaurant .com; Southern/Soul; $. Literally a stone's throw and across the street from **EVO** (see p. 91), Aunt Bea's is figuratively transported from another world and another time. With pencils behind ears and notepads in hand, the matronly, friendly staff here speaks to a different generation when fried chicken, cornbread, and sweet tea were not only mandatory, they were politically correct. Thank goodness for that! Aunt Bea's plentiful, stick-to-your-ribs meat 'n' three specials menu revolves daily (though fried chicken is always on the menu) and is served Monday through Friday, lunch only. The dining room is almost always full of a medley of blue collars and professionals digging into Aunt Bea's authentic Southern food.

North Charleston's colorful mayor Keith Summey is a regular here, where he sups on his wife's, owner Deborah Summey's, fine fare.

The Eclectic Chef, 125 Central Ave., Summerville, SC 29483; (843) 821-7733; www.eclecticchef.net; Soup/Sandwiches; $. Most aptly named, The Eclectic Chef is just that, eclectic. A gourmet-to-go, lunch, and dessert hot-spot situated on the pedestrian-only stretch of "Short" Central Avenue in the historic district, The Eclectic Chef is a little bit of all things delicious to all people. Executive Chef-Owner Ben McCollum ditched a high-profile business career for a toque, following his passion and talent into this small, bustling kitchen and a personal-chef career. Gutsy wraps and sandwiches are kissed with international influences, especially Italy, France, and the Mediterranean. House-made salads, casseroles, and tempting house-made cakes are on display for all to see at the front counter to set the greedy appetite wheels in motion for the likes of a French dip panini with a Cabernet au jus for dipping or a Frito pie, a kind of glorified nachos treat where chili and beans are served over corn chips and topped with melting cheddar and cool sour cream. Bistro chairs and small round tables on the inside invite a friendly neighborhood clientele while outside seating is available for a sunny day.

Eileen's Restaurant, 10597 Dorchester Rd., Summerville, SC 29483; (843) 832-4841; www.eileensrestaurant.com; Eclectic; $$. With its relatively bland, strip-mall exterior, equally bland interior, and remote location on Dorchester Road on the south side of

Summerville, it might seem wise to dismiss Eileen's. Don't make that mistake! If you're in these parts, it's worth a visit for lunch or dinner to savor the high-impact flavor of the Italian/continental menu here. A family affair in both the back and the front

of the house, Eileen's pulses with a sense of goodwill and real talent in the kitchen coming from chef Sean Sheehan and chef Ron Jarosch. Begin with the sizzling olives served in a bath of olive oil, fresh thyme and garlic. The beet salad crackles with freshness and gets added bite from the toasted goat cheese and peppery arugula. Simple but delicious, the rigatoni *buttera* is tossed with peppery sausage, sweet peas, and a creamy tomato sauce. Entree options are diverse and include braised lamb shanks, pork schnitzel, and a Thai BBQ salmon. Pasta portions can be ordered in full or half portions.

EVO, 1075 E. Montague Ave., Park Circle in North Charleston, SC 29405; (843) 225-1796; www.evopizza.com; Pizza; $$. Who would have thought that a tiny, mobile, wood-fired oven cart would have morphed into the thriving Neapolitan pizza and locavore dining destination that this is in less than 5 years? It should be no surprise though, really. From the beginning, EVO's owners have always put their money and their mission where their mouths are and it's spelled *local.* Early supporters of sourcing local farmers and produce, today the sunny-hued restaurant leads the fresh-taste parade with twice-daily prepared house mozzarella, house-made breads, slow-cooked sauces from the freshest tomatoes, and house-made sweet

Park Circle

Located in the historic district of North Charleston, this neighborhood is an ultra-scenic, almost Mayberry-esque series of side streets flanking the more industrial side of North Charleston, or North Chuck, as locals call it. Park Circle's nascent days occurred during World War II with the Charleston Navy Yard. In the past decade, the area has been undergoing a major renaissance with the addition of several environmentally conscious eateries and a general fervor of local pride. East Montague Avenue runs through the heart of it all, with Old World street lamps, brick-lined streets, and modest, beautifully tended homes largely occupied by young, forward-thinking professionals and families.

sausage (with light notes of fennel and sage) prepared daily. The pizzas, lightly sauced and topped discs of chewy, doughy, smoky, dough, are stunners, but don't stop there. Salads, especially the local Bibb lettuce salad (when in season), decorated with slivers of radishes and chives with a decadent blue cheese dressing, and fat, creatively compiled (but never complicated) panini, also shine cleanly and brightly here. Colorful local art adorns the walls, and the dining room and outside patio bustle with the positive energy of EVO devotees. The name is an acronym for Extra Virgin Oven. Add an "L" to the end, and it spells *love* in reverse. I promise you you'll fall in love with EVO. Not to be missed, the pistachio pesto pizza, a nutty ode to three cheeses drizzled with house-made crème fraîche (it's even better if you add the house-made sausage) will break your heart in the best of all possible ways.

Matt's Burgers, 102 S. Cedar St., Summerville, SC 29483; (843) 821-1911; Burgers; $. Funky, friendly, and tiny, Matt's serves big— make that huge—hand-rolled burgers seasoned with fresh onions, in this bright, clean location in the heart of downtown Summerville. There is even a "Bomb Hall of Fame" where those brave many who have sampled the Bomb—a whopper of a burger topped with American cheese, hot pepper cheese, 8 ounces of chili, mustard, pickle and fried onions—sign their names and leave their happy comments. Spanish fries, perky and hot and fried with onions and jalapeños, are a house favorite. Same goes for the Spanish fried okra, which is treated the same way. Matt's is not for the faint of heart. Bring a big appetite for their very gently priced, heaping plates of Americana with a dash of Spanish seasoning.

Perfectly Frank's, 118 N. Main St., Summerville, SC 29483; (843) 871-9730; Hot Dogs; $. Frank Cuda Sr. came to this country from Italy in 1910 and set up shop in Pittsburgh selling franks to support his siblings and his father—so began Cuda's Hot Dogs. The family frank tradition continues at this recently expanded gourmet frank, taco, and burger parlor. Nearly everything on the menu has a "Frank" moniker such as the Frank Morgan (a dog topped with cheesy, gooey mac 'n' cheese) to the Aretha (Frank)lin (a dog topped with pulled pork, barbecue sauce, slaw, and crispy onions). Like **Matt's** (p. 93), toss the calorie and cholesterol counter out the window here and dig in to some seriously delicious chow. For weight damage control, try the soft shrimp tacos heaping with grilled shrimp and topped with crunchy cabbage tossed with lime, an avocado lime aioli, and a fruit salsa, and call it a happy day.

The Perfect Wife, 131 Central Ave., Summerville, SC 29483; (843) 832-7737; www.theperfectwifesummerville.com; Eclectic; $. "Hungry?" That's what a large blackboard hung over the back wall of this darling coffee, catering, and cuisine corner asks all who enter the domain of The Perfect Wife. If you're not upon entering, you will be soon. The stomach rumbling aroma of dark, roasted coffee wafts throughout the small space, located just a few doors down from **The Eclectic Chef** (see p. 90). The Perfect Wife feels more feminine, with bright colors and soft, deep sofas for noshing and reading. The menu is not over-the-top-original, with standard dishes like black-bean soup with cilantro sour cream, or a French chicken salad tossed with mayonnaise, almonds, fresh tarragon, and "other secret ingredients". Maybe that's the key to The Perfect Wife? She adds just a dash of mystery and seduction in secret ingredients prepared with love to keep hubby and you coming back for more. If so, The Perfect Wife has mastered the art. And don't you just love the name?

Sesame Burgers & Beer, 4726 Spruill Ave. in Park Circle, North Charleston, SC 29405; (843) 554-4903; www.sesameburgersandbeer .com; Burgers; $. **Five Loaves Cafe** (see p. 67) divided and multiplied to add this hormone-free, ground-in-house burger joint to its already impressive restaurant résumé. At Sesame, it's all about fresh buns (sesame, of course), house-made condiments, and bring-it-on beef. Like Five Loaves, Sesame is vegetarian friendly—burgers can be made with beef, chicken, turkey, or black beans, and each receives your pick of a slew of lovely fresh slathering sauces from house-made ketchup and mayo to chipotle BBQ sauce or a flavor-packed basil pesto. Sesame's burgers are stacked and come with a refreshing side of house-made bread-and-butter pickles. Round those out with a stack of made-to-order sweet-potato fries or a house salad made with fresh, local produce. The ultimate grilled cheese is a thing of cheese-lovers' beauty. Thick sourdough gets stuffed with cheddar, brie, fontina, tomatoes, and a layer of garlic aioli and then is grilled until it all merges together in smooth, cheesy goodness, best when dipped in Sesame's house-made ketchup. Located a few blocks from Montague Avenue East, Sesame, as the name implies, is also a popular watering hole where locals soak up a 60-strong selection of brews ranging from lagers to stouts. A second location was recently added at the Citadel Mall at 2070 Sam Rittenberg Blvd. in West Ashley; (843) 766-7770.

Bertha's Kitchen, 2332 Meeting St., North Charleston, SC 29405; (843) 554-6519; Southern/Soul; $. Bertha's garish pink and purple/ blue cinder-block self, sitting on a little traveled stretch of North Meeting Street, could halt even color-blind traffic. Instead, Bertha's brings them in droves, from all walks of life, for soul food that makes them swoon with delight. Bertha's no longer living, but her knack for down-to-the-bone-flavor cooking lives on through her daughters, who work the kitchen. Fried chicken, stewed cabbage full of pink, smoky, fatty pork, stewed field peas, cheesy soft mac 'n' cheese with a crunchy, slightly burnt top, fried pork chops, and more all speak to the heart and soul of Southern soul cooking at its best. Prices are cheap, lines are long (get there before noon if you can), and food is served on Styrofoam plates—but Bertha's is an experience that will live on in your mind forever. Note: Bertha's is cash only. Bring the green!

The Dining Room at The Woodlands/The Pines, 125 Parsons Rd., Summerville, SC 29483; (843) 308-2115; www.woodlandsinn .com; American/Continental; $$$$. Situated on sprawling estate grounds anchored with a statuesque old inn, this address is only one of six properties in North America to hold both the Forbes' Five-Star and AAA's Five-Diamond rating for both food and lodging. The Dining Room's kitchen has been home to several decorated chefs including Ken Vedrinski (see **Trattoria Lucca,** p. 83) and Nate

Whiting (see **Tristan,** p. 55) The Inn's new owners have lightened up the formality of the dining experience here (including the new, more casual Pines dining area) and the daytime prices, while maintaining The Dining Room's stellar reputation. I love The Dining Room best for lunch, where sun streams through the huge windows overlooking the grounds and the quiet embrace of soft, floral upholstery and a glass of wine cushion the afternoon with a lingering lunch and the promise of a late afternoon nap chaser back at home. The Maine lobster BLT is full of huge chunks of sweet lobster barely cloaked in a citrus-infused tarragon mayonnaise and salty bacon wrapped up neatly with fat, Texas-sized brioche toast, or indulge in the exquisite Bibb lettuce salad dressed with more bacon, sweet, mild blue cheese, toasted cashews, and a soothing buttermilk dressing. Lunch also is the time to indulge in the 3-course business lunch for just $31. Expect to pay more, way more, for a la carte dining options or the tasting menu in The Dining Room. Service and wine pairings from a stellar wine list are, as to be expected given the property's well-earned rating status, as good as it gets around here.

Oscar's, 207 W. 5th North St., Summerville, SC 29483; (843) 871-3800; www.oscarsofsummerville.com; Eclectic; $$. Oscar's has been under the same ownership following the same casual elegance and eclectic menu game plan for over 25 years in a food town that's grown increasingly competitive. Part of the enduring appeal has to be the clubby, almost hunting lodge–like, dimly-lit setting that somehow seems to say "casual" and "elegant" all at once. It's the type of place that draws prom queens and kings as much as retirees who come for Oscar's chunky shrimp and grits (with a bewitching dash of Tabasco) or a classic Steak Oscar, topped off with crab meat, asparagus, and hollandaise sauce. Much of the menu follows classic, slightly old fashioned lines, but then it dances surprisingly off to the Southwest with a series of burritos and chimichangas. The food here is not expertly executed, but it is filling, reliable, and reasonable, a little bit like the old neighborhood friend and dining landmark Oscar's has become. Oscar's serves lunch, dinner, and brunch.

Specialty Stores, Shops, Markets & Producers

Accent on Wine, 132 Main St., Summerville, SC 29483; (843) 832-1212; Wine Shop. **Woodland's** (see p. 96) long-standing and celebrated former sommelier Stephane Peltier recently opened this charming wine and cheese shop in historic downtown Summerville. The France native personally selects the shop's wine and other goodies, including a dizzying, fragrant array of cheeses. Inventive wine and food tastings are regularly on tap, including rogue beer tastings, charcuterie tastings, assorted wine tastings (of course), and even tango nights.

Cherie's Specialty Meats & Cajun Cafe, 1005 Tanner Ford Blvd., Unit 104, Hanahan, SC 29410; (843) 797-2441; www.cheries specialtymeats.com; Specialty Foods/Cajun. Cherie's brings an authentic bite of the bayou directly to the Lowcountry at this cheery, Cajun grocery and cafe. The freezer shelves are stocked with gumbo, jambalaya, étouffée, andouille, tasso, boudin, and other imported Cajun claims to culinary fame. Of these, the most elaborate are the stuffed, boned meats, including the celebrated Tur-Duc-Ken—a boned chicken inside a boned duck inside a boned turkey—stuffed with your pick of Cajun kick, frozen and ready to bake at  home. Cherie's delightful little cafe is open 7 days a week, serving big-flavored Cajun lunches of tender beef tips with corn *maque choux*, muffulettas, and more.

COAST Brewing Company, 1250 2nd St. N., North Charleston, SC 29405; (843) 343-4727; www.coastbrewing.com; Craft Beer. A brew-impassioned duo operates this brewery located on the Old Navy Base in North Charleston. Local ingredients, bio-friendly (the brewery is run on waste feedstock biodiesel), and delicious, creative, craft brews are their shared mission. Several different and original beers are crafted on an ongoing basis. The brewery is open for tastings and tours on Thursday and Saturday (visit the website for time and details). No reservations required. Cash only, please.

gRAWnolaville, 5805 Campbell St., Hanahan, SC 29410; (843) 225-2983; www.grawnola.com; Specialty Food. Holistic chef Ken Immer is the type of guy you see walking around the farmers' market in a funky hat drinking a vat of green juice. A huge believer in raw foods and healthy living, he has taken these beliefs  to the next level with the success of his truly delicious (and good for you) gRAWnola bars and nuggets. A raw, gluten-free blend of seeds and nuts including pumpkin seeds, almonds, walnuts, apples, buckwheat, raisins, cinnamon, and more, the bars are made at the plant in Hanahan and sold at retailers up and down the Eastern seaboard. The food can also be purchased directly from the website.

H & L Asian Market, 5300-1 Rivers Ave., North Charleston, SC 29405; (843) 745-9365; www.hnlasianmarket.com; Specialty Food Shop/Asian. This huge Asian surprise lurks half-hidden, in bold red-and-white colors off of busy Rivers Avenue in this relatively industrial part of North Charleston. It's worth a look for hardcore fans of all things Asian, such as fresh, whole fish presented on glimmering beds of shaved ice, row after row of specialty Asian ingredients, and Asian cookware and utensils, from woks to chopsticks. All that shopping got you hungry? Check out the good eats at the authentic

Vietnamese restaurant located within the store. Delicious meatball and brisket pho, egg noodle soups, and assorted rice dishes are filling and moderately priced. The restaurant is cash only. The store is open 7 days a week.

Mepkin Abbey, 1098 Mepkin Abbey Rd., Moncks Corner, SC 29461; (843) 761-8509; www.mepkinabbey.org; Specialty Foods. Verdant, rolling hills and sweeping vistas of live oaks and moss surround the open grounds and farmland of this beautiful abbey settled by Roman Catholic monks on the historic grounds of the Mepkin Plantation. The monks cultivate milky, velvety, and delicious oyster mushrooms, which are sold locally to restaurants and via farmers' markets. Their sales help sustain the abbey. Visit the Mepkin Abbey Store on the grounds of the abbey to find the mushrooms in their dried and powdered form to stir into soups and stews. Here, you can also find "delectables" produced at this monastery and others around the world like creamed honey, Fr. Joe Tedesco's famous poppy-seed dressing, and "Drizzzle," a sweet and tangy fruit-juice syrup that's a perfect topper on anything from pancakes to pork. While you're here, indulge in a tour of the Mepkin Abbey Church or visit the exquisite Nancy Bryan Luce Gardens.

East of the Cooper: Mount Pleasant, Sullivan's Island, Daniel Island & Isle of Palms

Mount Pleasant and these other breezy beach and island communities lie, literally, east of the Cooper River. Two big bridges, either the Don N. Holt on I-526 or the Arthur Ravenel Jr. Bridge on Highway 17, will land you on two different ends of Mount Pleasant, while a few other smaller, scenic bridges are required to get to Sullivan's Island, Daniel Island, and Isle of Palms. The easy accessibility, marsh-enveloped beauty, and broad, sandy beaches of this entire side of greater Charleston have led to explosive growth, not just in the population, but in the quality and number of restaurants, eateries, and boutiques that sate a growing hunger for delicious food outside of downtown. Talented chefs like **Red Drum**'s Ben Berryhill (see p. 114) and **Langdon's** Patrick Langdon Owens (see p. 112) have responded in kind with first-class fare so enticing that both regularly attract clientele from all over town. Meanwhile, the nostalgic, beach-appropriate charm of **Jack's Cosmic Dogs** (see p. 112) or **Poe's Tavern**'s (see p. 107) fish tacos and juicy burgers have timeless, irresistible appeal, especially after a day at the beach.

Foodie Faves

Bacco Italian Restaurant, 976 Houston Northcutt Blvd., Ste. O, Mount Pleasant, SC 29464; (843) 884-6969; www.baccocharleston .com; Italian; $–$$. Menu simplicity combined with fresh ingredients, kitchen talent, and a good habit of never complicating his food have put Bacco's chef-owner Michael Scognamiglio on the top of the Mount Pleasant best dining destinations heap. All that, plus easy prices and a romantic, subdued, candlelit hush and it's easy to understand why Bacco is one of the best. Located in a busy strip mall just over the bridge from downtown, Bacco seamlessly transports guests to rustic Italy via soulful dishes like *ragù* Bolognese, and seared swordfish topped with sunny capers, raisins, and pine nuts. Scognamiglio takes obvious pleasure in pleasing his guests, and can often be seen overseeing his audience as a young father would his children or saying hushed hellos as he humbly makes his way through the 20 tables that mark the center of his beautiful Bacco world.

Crave Kitchen & Cocktails, 1968 Riviera Dr., Mount Pleasant, SC 29466; (843) 884-1177; Eclectic; $$–$$$. Situated deep into Mount Pleasant, near the Isle of Palms Connector in the Shoppes at Seaside Farms, Crave hits the spot for tasty, fresh, well-prepared food, cool drinks, and a neighborhood good time. Very dark and cavernous, Crave nonetheless resonates with locals for its consis-

tently good food. The menu mixes it up with the likes of coconut rings, brie bites, fish taco salads, and other riffs on bar food themes, but then steps up to the plate with adult-style goodness in the entrees that merge ingredients from all over the globe, in particular the Mediterranean. The hummus plate is one of Crave's unexpected shining stars. Beware of loudness coming from the bar on busy nights. Better to take a seat near the back and settle into one of the deep booths.

Dragon Palace Chinese Bistro, 162 Seven Farms Dr., Ste. 320, Daniel Island, SC 29492; (843) 388-8823; www.dragonpalacesc .com; Chinese; $$. I've probably eaten at Dragon Palace 10 times over the years, and every time I've enjoyed it. Not because the food is off-the-charts great, but because it is good, especially the dim sum, which comes in second place to downtown's excellent **O-Ku** (p. 72) for best dim sum in greater Charleston. The pork dumplings and roast pork buns shine especially brightly in the taste department and come served with a smile on pretty trays with tantalizing dipping sauces. However, the best reason to make the drive out to Daniel Island (about 25 minutes from downtown) is the way Dragon Palace looks. The entire dining room was constructed in Taiwan of marble and dark, beautiful woods, then broken down, shipped to Charleston, and reconstructed to create the imperial Qing Dynasty effect of the place. Kids young and old will love it for that alone. Speaking of kids, there is a nice children's menu and gluten-free, heart-healthy, and vegetarian options abound for adults.

Graze, 863 Houston Northcutt Blvd., Mount Pleasant, SC 29464; (843) 606-2493; www.grazecharleston.com; Eclectic; $–$$. As green as a just-watered field and as fresh as a daisy, Graze is an inviting new restaurant nook in Mount Pleasant that exudes friendliness and embraces all things organic. It's a relatively low-cost alternative for a high-style meal this side of the Cooper, and is just minutes from downtown. Portions are not for the faint of heart—no one goes away hungry here! Especially if you choose to indulge in the decadent lobster and mac 'n' cheese starter, which is hearty enough to easily serve four people. Same goes for fat, grass-fed burgers and sturdy, hungry man–style sandwiches like the prime rib topped with fried onions and horseradish cream sauce. Salads are stellar and served with lip-smacking tart/sweet house-made dressings. Art by local artists is showcased simply on the green walls and

The Mount Pleasant Farmers' Market

Mount Pleasant Farmers' Market Pavilion, 645 Coleman Blvd., at the Moultrie Middle School Grounds, Mount Pleasant, SC 29464; www.townofmountpleasant.com; Farmers Market; $. The recently constructed covered pavilion and paved grounds at this family-friendly farmers' market make for a rain-free, easygoing shopping experience, regardless of the weather. All local and food-focused, this festive market runs from April to October, on Tuesday afternoon starting at 3:30 and operating until dark, which usually means sometime between 7 and 8 p.m. Live music and oodles of delicious food (from many of the same vendors you'll see at the **Charleston Farmers' Market,** p. 85) make it a popular after-school stop for young families and professionals on the prowl for good times and good, locally raised eats.

makes for an eye-soothing view. Parking is ample and easy. Stroll over to Whole Foods Market across the parking lot after lunch or dinner to walk off your meal while combing the beautifully arranged aisles for an after-meal treat or bottle of wine.

High Thyme Cuisine, 2213-C Middle St., Sullivan's Island, SC 29842; (843) 883-3536; Eclectic; $$$. Neighbors dining and drinking at **Poe's** (p. 107) across the street, could probably tap your shoulder with their beer bottle necks, these establishments are so close. And not just in location, but also in theme. Like Poe's, High Thyme is beach-relaxed but definitely has more of an island bistro feel. The lighting is dim with lots of candles and not a small amount of romance. Quiet and casually sophisticated, High Thyme has a little bit of everything on the menu, and is particularly fish-intensive. The PEI mussels in a coconut-chili broth are stellar, and a house favorite. Other great bets include the earthy, roasted half chicken with acorn squash or the sweet, crunchy pan-seared scallops over truffled parsnip puree. Tapas Tuesday rocks the little house down with huge flavors in small-plate versions of many of the house favorites. The surf and sand are just feet away for a romantic après dinner stroll along the white/grey sands of sexy, sleepy Sullivan's Island.

Poe's Tavern, 2210 Middle St., Sullivan's Island, SC 29482; (843) 883-0083; www.poestavern.com; Burgers/Fish Tacos; $. The "tell-tale" hearts of burger and beach lovers everywhere beat loudly at Poe's, a beach bungalow tucked in the heart of historic Sullivan's Island and inspired by Edgar Allan Poe, who once lived on the island and wrote "The Gold-Bug" there during his stay. Sea breezes run through the small house, which is decked with cool bits of Poe para-phernalia and plenty of black raven silhouettes. Despite the dark theme, the mood here is always cheerful and beach-friendly. Cold brews flow freely from the taps situated near the long bar. Burgers can be prepared with either certified Angus chuck beef that's ground in-house or with a chicken breast filet and then topped with a vast array of fresh condiments. Burgers are named after Poe's published works (The Pit & Pendulum is a house favorite, topped with applewood bacon and cheddar). Despite Poe's burger fame, don't overlook the fish tacos—they're spot-on delicious and served with crunchy cabbage and creamy toppings. Beautiful Sullivan's Island beaches are just steps away, for an inviting after-lunch or dinner stroll. Ample outside seating is available.

The Square Onion, 18-B Resolute Ln., I'ON Square, Mount Pleasant, SC 29464; (843) 856-4246; www.squareonion.com; Gourmet-to-Go Meals/Soups/Sandwiches; $–$$. Husband-and-wife owners Mary and Cary Zapatka are committed to getting home-cooked meals on busy peoples' tables. There is no excuse not to do just that at this bright little take 'n' bake shop on the edge of the Stepford Wives-esque I'On village in Mount Pleasant. Pretty moms scoot their well-dressed children about this cheery, suburban neighborhood, which is designed to resemble downtown Charleston's historic district. Satisfying casseroles (don't miss the beefy, cheesy, delicious hamburger tater tot casserole), quiches, tomato pie, stacked, freshly made sandwiches, soups, and prepared salads are prettily displayed in the glass counter. A unique wine selection is also available to wash everything down with style. A second location recently opened nearby at 411 Coleman Blvd., Mount Pleasant, SC 29464; (843) 416-8684.

Stack's Coastal Kitchen, 1440 Ben Sawyer Blvd., Ste. 1107, Mount Pleasant, SC 29464; (843) 388-6968; www.stackscoastalkitchen.com; Gourmet-to-Go Meals/Soups/Sandwiches; $. A tad more down-home than **The Square Onion** (above), Stack's nonetheless offers similarly tasty goods. Both dish out succulent take-home treats, but those at Stack's are gutsier, a little less refined, and (like at The Square Onion), are generously stacked with really good, creative stuff, like the deep-dish deliciousness of the Denver omelet casserole or beef lasagna. But it's the sandwiches that rule here with a long list of big-flavored options on fresh bread or wraps with all the trimmings. The moist, tender, house-roasted chicken is a local favorite.

Landmarks

Atlanticville, 2063 Middle St., Sullivan's Island, SC 29482; (843) 883-9452; www.atlanticville.net; Southern/Seafood; $$$. Of all the restaurants we'll visit on Sullivan's Island in this book, Atlanticville is one of the oldest, in existence for nearly two decades. It's a wind- and sand-worn bungalow just feet from the beach on a quiet stretch of Middle Street, but Charleston native and chef-owner Bill

Condon keeps it as fresh as day one, if only better seasoned. His culinary riff is all Lowcountry, but he bastes it with international flavors and restrained classic French technique in dishes like Meyer's Ranch strip steak with hoppin' John risotto and tomato-ginger ranch gravy. The dining room feels relaxed, sophisticated, and slightly worn in, like a soft, cozy slipper. The theme is nautical and the tables are white linen–lined. Atlanticville's popular Thai night features an all-Thai menu and live music every Tuesday evening on the screened front porch where fun folks get their Thai on.

The Boathouse at Breach Inlet, 101 Palm Blvd., Isle of Palms, SC 29451; (843) 886-8000; www.boathouserestaurants.com; Seafood; $$–$$$. Featuring gorgeous remote views of wind-swept, turbulent Breach Inlet (which connects the Intracoastal Waterway and Isle of Palms), The Boathouse is the place to be for unfettered, fresh seafood. The setting is as rustic as the view in this former bait shop turned restaurant. Executive Chef Charles Arena is an ardent believer in two things: fresh, locally sourced fish and minimalist, classical cooking technique. Both shine here in crab fritters, roasted corn and crab soup, pan-roasted sea scallops with Parmesan risotto and lemon-rosemary vinaigrette, fried seafood platters, and selections from the fish board that rotate daily and can be prepared from a series of choices and with a selection of sides, including the restaurant's deservedly celebrated blue cheese coleslaw. Because the Isle of Palms (better known as IOP) is a popular home/condo rental destination for tourists and families during the summer months, it tends to attract a lot of (potentially loud) kids during early dining hours. Adults can find a silent, sea-breeze escape at the rooftop Crow Bar for a cool, soothing cocktail before or after dinner.

Huck's Lowcountry Table, 1130 Ocean Blvd., 2nd Floor, Isle of Palms, SC 29451; (843) 886-6772; www.huckslowcountrytable.com; Southern; $$$. Combine the rare restaurant ocean views of Front Beach on Isle of Palms, the passion and talent of local-source-focused Executive Chef-Owner JJ Kern, and minimalist manipulation of beautiful produce from Four Corner Farms in Dorchester County, and you have the makings for a landmark East Cooper dining destination. And since the sexy, nautical-themed space opened in 2008, that's what Huck's has become. The large, geometrically shaped white plates showcase simple, delicious dinners like goat-cheese toast with arugula pesto and white-balsamic marinated tomatoes. Or go deep South, with a smashing rendition of buttermilk fried chicken served alongside mashed sweet potatoes with stewed collards and sage, with sausage pan gravy. Honey-toned woods, and plays on stark white and ocean blue dress up the intimate yet spacious dining room with the cooling shades of the sea.

Huck's also serves lunch during peak season, starting in the spring.

Jack's Cosmic Dogs, 2805 Hwy. 17 N., Mount Pleasant, SC 29464; (843) 884-7677; www.jackscosmicdogs.com; Hot Dogs; $. *The Jetsons* meets *Happy Days* in the happiest of all ways at Jack's far-out hot dog adventure land. Revisit the kid in you at Jack's, which is outfitted with all kinds of retro nods to the '50s and '60s, including a space-age rocket logo and NeHi sodas. All dogs have cosmic monikers and all-beef goodness, whether it's the signature "Cosmic Dog" topped with a crisp, cool slaw graced with just the right amount of blue cheese and slathered with house-made sweet-potato mustard or the "Mercury Meatloaf" in a bun. It's always good and always fun at Jack's. Wash down your dog with a draft root beer or frothy, thick milk shake or malt made with custard soft-serve ice cream. The newest location is situated on the way out to surfer-central Folly Beach and takes on the beach theme with surfboard seating and an even bigger, brighter look that's perfect for an après beach hunger whipping. It can be found at 1531 Folly Beach Rd. on James Island; (843) 225-1817.

Langdon's Restaurant and Wine Bar, 778 S. Shelmore Blvd., Mount Pleasant, SC 29464; (843) 388-9200; www.langdonrestaurant .com; Eclectic; $$$. A former jock and musician and Charleston native with no formal training but a love of good food and cooking, Executive Chef-Owner Patrick Langdon Owens turned his unlikely restaurant dreams into a reality when he opened Langdon's nearly a decade ago. Arguably one of the top three chefs this side of town, Owens really understands the importance of using the best products and treating them with care and just the right amount of flair—

but never too much. The food is remarkable here and takes Owens' minimalist, international cues with tasty vigor, whether it's a simple daily cheese plate with local wildflower honey or the stunning seared diver scallops served with sweet-corn cream and basil oil. Beef comes big and beautiful here on pretty plates and big (but not off the charts) price tags. The setting, with ample, crisp black-and-white contrasts and dim lighting, feels very chic yet comfortable. Add the fabulous wine list and professional staff, and Langdon's is perfect for a romantic dinner for two or a quiet business dinner. Langdon's is the only restaurant in Mount Pleasant to currently hold the AAA Four Diamond Award.

Old Village Post House, 101 Pitt St., Old Village, Mount Pleasant, SC 29464; (843) 388-8935; www.mavericksouthernkitchens.com; Southern; $$–$$$. Pitt Street is one of the sweetest, Mayberry-esque streets you could ever hope to meet. Complete with an old-school soda fountain at the pharmacy, it just oozes with Victorian, small-town charm. And at the top of Pitt sits Old Village Post House, also known as OVPH. A cousin to **S.N.O.B.** (p. 53) downtown and a member of Maverick Southern Kitchens restaurant group, OVPH is located in a former mail post and doubles as a bed-and-breakfast and tavern. Amped with Southern swagger (there is even a large mural of Rhett and Scarlett on the white bead-board walls) and gentility, the space is small, quiet, and romantic under the breezy caress of whirring paddle-board fans. Executive Chef Frank Lee oversees the tiny, open kitchen that regularly produces bold, seasonal flavor. The shrimp and grits, pregnant with Cajun goodness in andouille sausage and country ham, is one of the best versions in town. Or, consider crispy braised pork served with collards, white lima beans, and a bourbon molasses reduction. Brunch is lovely here, especially if weather permits seating on the pretty outside porch area.

Red Drum, 803 Coleman Blvd., Mount Pleasant, SC 29464; (843) 849-0313; www.reddrumrestaurant.com; Southwestern/Southern; $$–$$$. Pint-sized dynamo Executive Chef-Owner Ben Berryhill brings Texas to the Lowcountry at this deservedly popular and praised whitewashed adobe restaurant gem. A labyrinth of different rooms—from the lively bar to the wine room and the relaxed elegance of the dining room—provide the just-right setting to fit your exact mood. And, the food! Much of it is wood-fired and infused with the spice and heat of Texas cuisine, then tempered with Berryhill's amazing flavor and texture balancing abilities and the influence of Lowcountry ingredients (like the red drum fish the restaurant is named for) and seasonal produce. The sweet corn pudding, one of the best things you can ever hope to eat, comes bubbling and golden and smooth, floating in its own individual corn husk tamale. Lightly fried local shrimp is served with a fresh *salsa verde* and smoked chile and the beef short ribs braised in house barbecue sauce with cowboy beans and jalapeño cheese bread say Texas with a capital "T"! Live music is played in the festive (and often loud) bar, while outside dining by the adobe fireplaces affords a quieter, alfresco time. The wine list is excellent.

SeeWee Restaurant, 4808 N. Hwy. 17, Awendaw, SC 29429-5909; (843) 928-3609; Southern; $$. OK, it's a hike from downtown. You're looking at a good 45 minute ride well past the suburban boroughs of Mount Pleasant and past the "rural" sweetgrass basket-weaving corridor of Highway 17. But, let me tell you, it's worth it. A roadside stop of the highest Southern order, this former general store turned dining destination has been drawing crowds from all over for decades. Service is sweet from a fleet of aging, plump matrons who kindly begin every meal with a heaping basket of fryer-fresh, sweet, crunchy hush puppies. If you're lucky and smart, you'll end your meal with one of the house-made pies and cakes created in neighboring home kitchens by baking pros. The coconut cream pie is a taste of airy, real custard and whipped cream heaven. In between, fill up on fresh, local, and delicious fried seafood platters or vegetable plates of butter beans, rice and gravy, and mac 'n' cheese, if you please.

Vickery's Shem Creek Bar & Grill, 1313 Shrimp Boat Ln., Mount Pleasant, SC 29464; (843) 884-4440; www.vickerys.com; Burgers/Seafood; $$. Though the food is sturdy, filling, and solid here, it's the views that make it really come together in fine, Shem Creek fashion (see **Shem Creek—A Shrimping Tradition,** p. 117). Rustic shrimp boat rigs, glittering water views deep into the harbor, cooling breezes and gentle sunshine are a tough-to-resist combo paired with a big burger and a cold brew. Vickery's is a popular target for the brunch and Bloody Mary hangover crowd on Sunday afternoon. Burgers are your best bet here, though the black bean soup and jerk chicken plate are equally fair fare. If you have a boat and want dockside service, boaters are invited to tie up at Vickery's dock on a first come, first served basis.

The Wreck of the Richard & Charlene, 106 Haddrell St., Mount Pleasant, SC 29464; (843) 884-0052; www.wreckrc.com; Southern/Seafood; $$. Named after a trawler that washed up on the site of this Charleston restaurant institution during devastating Hurricane Hugo in 1989, The Wreck is pretty much just that. A true dive in the most charming sense of the word, the hard-to-find sea shack has wraparound views of marshes, water, and shrimping boats on Shem Creek (see sidebar, **Shem Creek—A Shrimping Tradition,** below). Screened, open windows invite salty, sea breezes and convivial, relaxed chatter over the bowl of boiled peanuts that begins every meal, washed down with a couple of ice-cold brews. The menu is almost pure seafood—fried shrimp, fried oysters, fried flounder—you name it. If it's fish and it's fresh, you'll find it at The Wreck. Sides include classic Southern staples like red rice and deviled crab. The Wreck's website offers excellent directions, thankfully. Follow them closely, and you will find it. Please note, the restaurant closes early—9:30 p.m. on weekends! Also, there is no children's menu.

SHEM CREEK—A SHRIMPING TRADITION

For hundreds of years, Shem Creek has served as shrimping central to local shrimpers and home base to the Magwood family fishing tradition. The blue waters and surrounding marsh, reaching out into the harbor and toward the Atlantic, still shimmer with the promise of shrimp, but significant declines in shrimping profitability and the profusion of restaurants here have limited the amount of shrimp actually delivered to these docks. Still, scenic shrimp boats with their majestic masts and fat, low bodies bob in the water for all to see and enjoy from restaurants like **Vickery's** (p. 115) and **The Wreck** (p. 116), seasoning every meal with nautical charm, salty air, and gorgeous scenery.

Specialty Stores, Markets & Producers

Callie's Biscuits, www.calliesbiscuits.com; Specialty Foods. Celebrated local caterer Callie White parlayed her cooking talents and business acumen into this spectacularly delicious specialty line of biscuits, pimento cheeses, and more. These days her daughter Carrie Morey is at the helm, cranking out the likes of ham biscuits, cinnamon biscuits, cheese and chive biscuits, cocktail ham biscuits, and more Southern-style, artisanal, flaky, delights at their Mount

Pleasant–based facility. The name may say biscuits, but bring on the cheese, pimento cheese that is. Chunky, slightly sweet with just enough heat, it's simply delicious eaten right out of the container, slathered on a warm biscuit, or on top of a fat burger. Callie's goods can be purchased online and are also available at specialty shops across the country. The biscuits are custom packaged and arrive frozen, ready to be re-heated fresh from the oven.

Laura Alberts Tasteful Options, 891 Island Park Dr., Daniel Island, SC 29492-7993; (843) 881-4711; www.lauraalberts.com; Cafe/Craft Beer/Wine; $$ (cafe). Yet another mother-and-daughter team makes good here, offering Southern specialties at the cafe-restaurant, as well as a select list of nearly 20 fine wines and a slew of craft beers that flow from a 6-tap growler station. The recipes come from Laura's kitchen (which also offers catering services) and feature simple, delicious items such as Laura's trio—crab dip, shrimp paste, and jalapeño pimento cheese and Laura's barbecue shrimp and grit cake with barbecue bourbon sauce.

Westbrook Brewing Company, 510 Ridge Rd., Mount Pleasant, SC 29464; (843) 708-2964; www.westbrookbrewing.com; Craft Beer/Brewery. Mount Pleasant's first microbrewery shimmers with modern lights and sleek counters. Its centrally located, circular bar and tasting room is a thing of beauty and the design makes for comfortable, easy sipping. The eco-friendly brewery creates several house brews that are served year-round, plus seasonal and experimental brews too. Tours are available with tastings on Thursday, Friday, and Saturday afternoons.

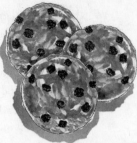

yesUmay Cookies, 280 W. Coleman Blvd., Mount Pleasant, SC 29464; (866) 986-6946; www.yesUmaycookies.com; Bakery. Go ahead and indulge your sweet tooth and step up some positive, guilt-free energy at this bright and cheerful bakery. Founder Ashley Swider employs organic, healthful ingredients like sea salt, curry, and goji berries in her whimsical, delicious cookies with happy names like Blissed Out, Fruitful Love, and Sweet Satisfaction. Her goal is to share her love of fresh-baked cookies with her rapidly growing clientele. Cookies can be purchased by the half dozen or dozen, or in a package of 24 mini cookies. The Sweet Satisfaction, one of the bakery's best sellers, looks like part of a wedding cake but is, in fact, a simple, flaky butter cookie topped with a fat swath of creamy buttercream. Silver or gold metallic sprinkles add pretty shimmer and toothsome crunch.

Learn to Cook

The Coastal Cupboard, 644 J Long Point Rd., Belle Hall Shopping Center, Mount Pleasant, SC 29464; (843) 856-4321; www.thecoastal cupboard.com; Cooking Store/Cooking School. People who love to cook will grow absolutely giddy perusing this cavernous, well-organized store that is stocked to the gills with state-of-the-art knives, cookware, luscious imported linens, spices, service ware and more. Basically, anything your little cooking heart desires! The staff is super friendly and helpful in directing visitors through the shop. In the rear, there is an attractive kitchen where cooking classes are held by in-house chef Amanda Johnson and visiting chefs from Charleston and elsewhere.

Janet Gaffney's The Art of Cooking, 20 Grace Ln., Mount Pleasant, SC 29464-2661; (843) 971-9281; Cooking School. Looking for a place for kids to burn youthful energy while they learn? Janet Gaffney's cooking school is dedicated to teaching healthful, joyful cooking to people of all ages, but her forte is kids. During summer months, Gaffney hosts several cooking camps for kids, ages 8 to teens, focusing on baking and regional and international cooking styles and ingredients.

James Island & Folly Beach

I once wrote that James Island is to James Islanders what Yankee Stadium is to New Yorkers—a source of extreme local pride that is fiercely, fiercely defended. Rightly so! Beautiful and diverse, the long, narrow island flanks the peninsula on the Ashley River side and is easily accessed via the large James Island Connector (which affords some of the best views of the harbor and city around) or the smaller bridge heading over the river on Highway 17 heading south. Just minutes from downtown, James Island (or JI as it's more commonly known) is light years away in mood and style. Rife with pockets of intimate suburbia, schools, and families, it stretches through a growing string of traffic congestion and restaurant options on Folly Road until ending at Folly Beach, also called "the Edge of America." There is exquisite marsh and water scenery before crossing the bridge into the bohemian surfing mecca of Folly Beach, where youthful, flip-flop-clad, surfboard-toting locals commingle with nature-loving tourists as merrily as crabs with sand. The dress and budgets are more relaxed all over the island, but culinary standards are not. There are some very good eats in these parts, well worth taking a short trip to savor.

Foodie Faves

Blu Restaurant & Bar, 1 Center St., Folly Beach, SC 29439; (843) 588-6658; www.BLUFollyBeach.com; Seafood/American Eclectic; $$–$$$. Cooling shades of aquatic blue tempered with beige upholstery and wide-open views of waves cresting and rolling into the white water and sand of Folly Beach unquestionably mark Blu as Folly's most sophisticated dining choice. Even though it's located in the lobby of a Holiday Inn, Blu is light years removed from the surfing, beach kitsch that surrounds it, affording an idyllic setting for a quiet, romantic dinner for two or a business lunch by the sea. The food, a largely seafood-oriented mix, has always been solid, but has recently stepped even closer to the sustainable seafood and high-quality cuisine plate in the hands of Executive Chef Jon Cropf. He employs restrained, classic technique and clean, uncluttered flavor pairings in dishes such as diver scallops over a puree of cauliflower with Fresno chili and Valencia orange or a loin of Kurobuta pork served with crispy bacon, baby carrots, Anson Mills grits, and sweet-tea barbecue sauce. Inventive specialty drinks taste especially nice when sipped after dinner on the outside patio, while sea breezes blow the day's cares away and set the stage for sweet dreams indeed. Blu also serves a popular Sunday brunch, as well as lunch, when the prices are decidedly gentler.

Brick House Kitchen, 1575 Folly Rd., James Island, SC 29412; (843) 406-4655; www.brickhousecharleston.com; Lowcountry/ Southern; $–$$. Settle into true familial graciousness at this lovely, rambling old farmhouse that sits on the original grounds of the Thomas family's homestead and plantation. Owned and operated by members of the same family, it charms and beguiles with grand-mother's antique collection of deviled-egg plates on the walls and delicious, locally sourced freshness on the table. Complete with a sunny, wraparound porch equipped with a massive community table and rocking chairs, the kitchen hums with simply prepared spe-cialties like shrimp cakes over brown rice, panfried salmon cakes, garden-fresh soups and salads, and a dizzying array of house-made cakes and pies beckoning from a large, clear-glass refrigerator case. Keep a close eye on the list of daily specials, which showcase the freshest of the fresh from local farms and gardens. A limited list of beer, wine, and cock-tails is available, along with sweet tea, of course. Look for a wall of old doors painted brick red just as you're passing the final turn in the road before it straightens out for a bee-line to Folly Beach, turn in, and welcome your own virtual home away from home.

The Drop In Bar & Deli, 32B Center St., Folly Beach, SC 29439; (843) 633-0234; www.dropindeli.com; Sandwiches/Salads; $. A youthful, hip energy permeates this surfboard-flagged restaurant, generously offering huge sandwiches heaping with freshness and best-quality ingredients. Drop In has a slight "granola" theme that's

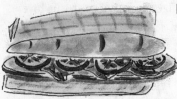

in perfect keeping with its Folly locale with healthy options like hummus, big leafy salads, and many veggie and gluten-free options. Meat eaters will revel in tooth-some treats like a warm roast beef French dip oozing in melting, gooey provolone and a savory au jus sauce, or the "Grooving Reuben," filled to its rye bread gills with corned beef, sauerkraut, and "comeback dressing" good-ness. Food is served from 11 a.m. to 10 p.m. daily and then the bar starts to thump with the beat of nightly live music and neighbor-hood cheer. A limited breakfast menu is served all day as well.

El Bohio at The Pour House, 1977 Maybank Hwy., James Island, SC 29412; (843) 571-4343; www.charlestonpourhouse.com; Cuban; $. Get ready for one of the biggest, most delicious taste sur-prises Charleston has to offer. El Bohio is off-the-charts packed with entirely authentic Cuban flavor and familial friendliness, to boot. Vanessa Harris is a Miami native with Cuban parents who happens to really, really know how to cook. Her mojo sauce, which drenches almost anything you like at this Havana-reinvented nook, is unfor-gettably fresh and delicious. A blend of fresh lime, olive oil, ample fresh garlic, and dried oregano, it's a fabulous flavor friend for the restaurant's equally fabled Cuban sandwich—lovingly marinated and roasted pork, with ham or turkey (your choice), garnished with a salty pickle and tangy mustard, all wrapped up in freshly baked, slightly sweet, dark Cuban bread. Harris's music-loving husband runs the live-music mecca, The Pour House, next door, but in my mind, the food is the reason to come, day or night. The *papas rellenas,* little balls of fried potatoes stuffed with fragrant ground beef will send your heart aflutter. They are that good, especially with some of that extra mojo for good measure!

J. Paulz!, 1739 Maybank Hwy., Ste. V, James Island, SC 29412; (843) 795-6995; www.jpaulz.com; Tapas/Sushi; $–$$. Feeling hungry, indecisive about what you want to eat, and in the mood for a good time? Target J. Paul'z! The menu borrows inspiration from all over the globe from Asia to Spain to the Lowcountry, particularly in the tapas departments. Small plates of truffled mac 'n' cheese prepared with a Spanish *queso,* white-truffle oil, and panko crust, brisket tacos, and tomato pie prepared with sweet Vidalia onions, fontina, and mozzarella in a crisp puff pastry just beg for one of the infused cocktails at J.Paulz!.

Larger appetites can turn to the traditional entree section of the menu, while sushi lovers have many fresh, hand-rolled options, as well. The dining area sort of rambles into several semiprivate nooks and crannies of low coffee tables with pillow-draped benches and soft sofas. There is an intimate outside patio seating area that twinkles with candlelight and youthful sophistication after dark.

Lost Dog Cafe, 106 W. Huron Ave., Folly Beach, SC, 29439; (843) 588-9669; www.lostdogfollybeach.com; Eclectic; $. Get your bow-wow on at this comfortable feeding post just off the main drag of Folly Beach's Center Street. The walls are decked with photos of furry friends, and water bowls greet thirsty pooches in for a break from the sun and fun. Seating for dogs is outside only on the sunny, airy patio. The food comes in big portions and with big, fresh flavors. Breakfast, with the likes of a bean-and-cheese quesadilla topped with a snappy salsa and all the fixings, including eggs and sour cream, is served all day. Big, crunchy bowls of salad, "Good Dog, Good Dog" Boar's Head all-beef hot dogs, and myriad wraps round out the fulfilling menu at this family-friendly spot that's especially popular for weekend breakfasts and brunch. Lunch is also a mainstay.

Rita's Seaside Grille, 2 Center St., Folly Beach, SC 29439; American Eclectic; $. The combined elements of sea breezes, sand, and surf have an uncanny ability to stir up hefty waterside appetites. Rita's, nestled just behind a large surf shop and a stone's throw from the sands of Folly Beach, resonates an easy beach groove that is tough to resist. A fluted tin roof, white bead-board paneling and ample breeze-kissed seating enhance Folly's colorful, mellow mood to a T. The menu includes a little bit of everything—crunchy, cool salads, fried seafood plates, and assorted starters with surf-themed

names like "Wipeout Chili"—but most people come to Rita's for their celebrated burgers, which include 10 choices, all priced at $10. The best seller, the Southbound burger with pimento cheese and apple-smoked bacon, presents a sizeable stack of gut-busting good-ness, especially when you tack on the heaping plate of hot, hand-cut French fries that comes with it. Dogs are wel-come on the back patio as long as they enter through the side gate, not the main restaurant. Weekday breakfasts and weekend brunches draw a large early-riser crowd, especially during beach season.

Savory Sushi & Catering, 1956-B Maybank Hwy., Charleston, SC 29412; (843) 762-3338; www.savorysushiandcatering.com; Sushi/Sandwiches/Gourmet-to-Go Meals; $. Next door to a small, indie movie theater, this fabulous little spot serves a little bit of every-thing and all of it is smashing, fresh, and with a healthy twist—including oodles of vegan and vegetarian alternatives. The sushi is out of this world and so are the sandwiches, but it's the ready-to-bake casseroles—beef stroganoff, shepherd's pie, seafood lasagna, Swedish meatballs, and a knockout tomato pie—that truly rock. Pick one up, bake it up at your rented beach house, and you've got a feast to remember to go with the soothing sounds of the surf.

Smoky Oak Taproom, 1234 Camp Rd., James Island, SC 29412; (843) 762-6268; www.smokyoak.com; Barbecue/Craft Beer; $. Cheap eats, heaping plates, and a selection of more than 40 craft beers served from the tap or by the bottle bring folks (especially 20- and 30-somethings) out in droves to this ramshackle watering hole located off a winding road at the far reaches of James Island. Fans of dry-rubbed, long-smoked ribs and brisket will have ample reason to smile at Smoky Oak, where both arrive warm, tender and delicious, just begging for one of several house-made sauces and a couple of comforting side dishes. Wood-grilled pizzas are another worthy option for hungry stomachs in search of good eats and a neighborhood good time.

Taco Boy, 15 Center St., Folly Beach, SC 29439; (843) 588-9761; www.tacoboy.net; Tacos/Mexican; $. Even though it's their second location, Taco Boy on Folly has a setting that's idyllically suited both to the beach mood and feisty food. With his snappy motto, "Skip Siesta, Let's Fiesta," Taco Boy (at both locations) departs from restaurant group REV's (see **Monza,** p. 71, **Closed for Business,** p. 65, and **Poe's Tavern,** p. 107) usually perfectly executed skill of combining a spectacular theme/setting with equally spectacular food. While the food is good here, honestly, it's not great. The guacamole, spiked with jalapeño, salt, pepper, and lime, is always chunky, cool, and fresh, and makes a tasty meal in itself with a bowl of chips and a trio of fresh salsas, and the tempura mahi-mahi taco with cilantro, red cabbage, and a cooling ancho chile yogurt sauce is satisfying. But Taco Boy's cool, extensive beer list and specialty drinks, including a pineapple-infused tequila margarita with hints of cinnamon and vanilla, will likely trump the food. In the end, it's the setting—dappled with Mexican antiques, forged metal, and colorful religious icons—that makes both Taco Boys worthy of a visit, especially refreshing after a long, thirsty day on the beach. The downtown location is on 217 Huger St.; (843) 789-3333.

Taco Spot, 1301 B Ashley River Rd., Charleston, SC 29407; (843) 225-7426; www.thetacospot.com; Tacos; $. One wouldn't necessarily expect some of the best tacos in Charleston, let alone the entire southeast, by just looking at "The Spot," as it's better known. Look for the huge orange dot at this tiny spot in an unsuspecting strip mall on Ashley River Road, and you've arrived.

Johnson & Wales grad and seasoned chef Jason C. Vaughan puts some serious chef "mustard" into the food here. The creamy sweet/hot house-made *queso* puts new meaning into the word "irresistible," and all the impeccable sauces are fresh, delicious, "real" and made in house. The Spot is most widely recognized for its fish tacos (grouper—blackened or seared), which are served with the lip-smacking-good likes of cilantro soy aioli or cayenne ranch. Tacos come wrapped either in a 6-inch soft flour shell or corn shells. What seem to be hundreds of bottled hot sauce options line the counter overlooking the kitchen, and beer flows freely and cold here. Vegetarian and kid-friendly options, including quesadillas, taco salads, burritos, and wraps ensure that there is literally something for everyone at Taco Spot.

Tokyo Crepes, 110 E. Ashley Ave., Folly Beach, SC 29439; (843) 513-5156; Crepes; $. Can't quite stomach the idea of a full-on sit-down meal on your day at the beach? Sashay your sarong over to Tokyo Crepes' psychedelically colored food truck for your fill of made-to-order crepes of both the sweet and savory variety. Former Portland, Oregon, resident and Japan native Yukari Yucca got turned on by the west coast's hot food truck scene and decided to bring it to Charleston, along with her friend John Baker. The versatility of crepes was a big part of the draw, and the flavorful, warm wraps, from Smoky Pork to Sweet Devil to the Cuban Crepe, have caught on here faster than a fire in a parched forest struck with a live flame. Tokyo Crepes seldom departs from this, their almost permanent location. Hours vary with the seasons. Check out their Facebook page or call ahead for seasonal updates.

Zia Taqueria, 1956-A Maybank Hwy., Charleston, SC 29412; (843) 406-8877; www.ziataco.com; Mexican/Southwestern; $. Another surprise find, Zia Taqueria is handily situated right next door to **Savory Sushi** (see p. 127). If your food mood is traveling south of the border, this is where to stop. Chef-Owner Kevin Grant spent some time in New Mexico and the Sandia Mountains honing his love and knowledge of Mexican cuisine. Orders are taken at the counter and large plates, heaping with food and flavor, are delivered to your cheerful black-and-yellow table. The "platos Mexicanos" are superb, and garnished with the creamiest Mexican *crema* to soothe the heat of fresh jalapeño relish, and counter the zesty bite of fresh lime and cilantro. The long-cooked beef barbacoa is full of spice and everything nice, with flavor deeply seeped in every bite. To wash it all down, select from an impressive array of made-to-order, perfectly mixed margaritas or a cold brew.

Landmarks

Bowens Island Restaurant, 1870 Bowens Island Rd., James Island, SC 29412; (843) 795-2757; www.bowensislandrestaurant .com; Seafood; $. Originally a fish camp founded in 1946, Bowens has morphed into one of greater Charleston's most celebrated seafood "dive" landmarks. The setting is ultra-casual, with oyster-shucking tables with round holes to chuck the shells and the smell of freshly roasting oysters in the air. Screened in and Southern down to the very last boiled peanut, Bowens is a must-do experience, especially on sultry summer evenings or slightly cool fall and winter evenings, when Lowcountry oysters are at their sweetest. A dusty dirt road brings you to the back door, just a few miles from the heart of Folly Beach.

Crosby's Fish & Shrimp Company, 2223 Folly Rd., James Island, SC 29412; (843) 795-4049; Seafood; $. Look for the pale-blue beach bungalow on wooden stilts on your right just before you cross the tiny bridge that takes you to Folly Beach, and you've found Crosby's. This long-standing family-run establishment lands fresh seafood daily, which they sell (along with beer, bait, and salty Southern charm) from an iced, fresh fish–laden counter. This is already a great thing, but add the warm weather Friday evening dock parties Crosby's hosts on the long dock behind the shop, and you've got a hands-down, authentic Lowcountry dining experience that won't break the bank, and might just break your heart, with those marsh views, fried fish, boiled shrimp, and ice-cold beer. Check in with Crosby's for seasonal hours for this not-to-be missed alfresco dining event. It changes every year, but generally is offered roughly from April until November, or when the weather gets very cold.

Mondo's Delite, 915 Folly Rd., James Island, SC 29412; (843) 795-8400; www.eatatmondos.com; Italian; $$. Nearly fifteen years ago, two recent Johnson & Wales grads decided they were going to open their own restaurant. Little by little, and against tough odds, the grads embraced their nascent business and cooking skills to make Mondo's the true delight that it still is, developing an almost immediate groundswell of loyal patrons in the process. They keep on coming for lunch and dinner, seeking the modestly priced, old-fashioned red-sauce Italian fare with a super-fresh and modern twist. Fish and fresh vegetables are prominent players on the expansive daily specials blackboard, while old-school Italian classics dominate the regular lunch and dinner menus. Beefy spaghetti and meatballs with a lovingly prepared, slightly sweet marinara, and cheesy, chewy baked ziti are favorites, but my dreams frequently turn to the heavenly eggplant Parmigiana, which is plated individually in a shallow, oval gratin dish and layered with breaded and fried eggplant, fresh tomatoes, plenty of cheese, and arrives at the table golden and bubbling over with deliciousness. The restaurant is long, narrow, and intimate, and service is always friendly and informed.

West Ashley & Points South, including Edisto Island

West Ashley is a sizeable tract of land that begins once you cross over the Ashley River on Highway 17 South from downtown, and continues quite a way west until you get to the historic plantations on Highway 61, finally petering out near Summerville. To the north, it's flanked by North Charleston, and to the south it extends toward the rural edges of Hollywood and Ravenel. Slightly farther south, off of Highway 17, is the turnoff to scenic Edisto Island, home to a smattering of delicious destinations (see **Po' Pigs Bo-B-Q,** p. 144 and **Geechie Boy Market and Mill,** p. 145) worth the nearly hour-long drive from downtown. This entire area has grown tremendously in recent years, both in population and, consequently, in the quality and diversity of restaurants and foodie faves. All of the destinations profiled in this short chapter are worth a visit when you're in the area, and some (particularly **The Glass Onion,** p. 141 and **Al di La,** p. 140) rival some of downtown's very best.

Foodie Faves

Caliente, 3669 Savannah Hwy., Johns Island, SC 29455; (843) 766-4416; www.calientecharleston.com; Mexican; $. The address states Johns Island, but this is technically in West Ashley and is the last feeding-worthy stop heading south on Savannah Highway (and still on the mainland) before you cross over the bridge to Johns Island or hit points further south on Edisto. Painted with colorful primary hues, the intimate space is chock full of authentic Mexican goodies. The pulled-pork or beef-brisket tacos, hard or soft shell, satisfy both the belly and the soul with Mexican rice, chunky black beans, and soothing melted-cheese garnishes. The creamy, slightly hot *queso* dip hits the mark with baskets of fresh tortillas and fresh tomato salsa. Service is fast but not hurried for a satisfying midday repast or dinner. It's a preferred haunt for the local food and beverage professionals in the area—you can usually spy one or two of them nibbling away in the quiet but fun ambience Caliente so graciously affords.

Fiery Ron's Home Team BBQ, 1205 Ashley River Rd., West Ashley, SC 29407; (843) 225-7427 and (843) 225-2278; www .hometeambbq.com; Barbecue; $. Chef-Owner Aaron Siegel took a big, brave step away from the security of a chef gig at one of Charleston's leading restaurants to open this jamming 'cue joint a few years ago. Covered with ruffled tin and a smokehouse patina, the former gas station comes alive daily with the scent of burning wood and cooking dry-rubbed pig. "Heavy Hitter" platters are stacked to order on plastic plates at the buffet line and come with your choice of two sides and Texas toast for good dipping in one of Home Team's winning house-made barbecue sauces. For my money, the golden mustard-vinegar sauce hits a home run. The ribs are to die for and go super nicely with the crunchy/smooth mac 'n' cheese and cucumber and tomato salad sides, in particular. Grab a

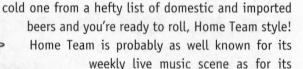

cold one from a hefty list of domestic and imported beers and you're ready to roll, Home Team style! Home Team is probably as well known for its weekly live music scene as for its 'cue. A new location, featuring table service and a slightly more expansive menu just opened at 2209 Middle St. on Sullivan's Island; (843) 883-3131.

Hubee D's, 975 Savannah Hwy., St. Andrew's Shopping Center, West Ashley, SC 29407; (843) 556-0330; www.hubeeds.com; Wings/ Fried Chicken; $. "Deelicious" is the motto at this wings and chicken tenders hot spot, and it's spot-on. Look beyond the slightly chain-like, yellow-and-red-plastic veneer, and you'll be glad you did. An antique red pickup truck parked just outside is the first clue to Southern, Charleston-native authenticity that drives Hubee's. The red plastic baskets brimming with plump, slow-smoked, and dry-rubbed wings and buttermilk-bathed, then thick batter-dipped chicken tenders, both fried to order, are the second and third. Dipped in any one of the impossibly delicious house-made sauces (except for the ubiquitous honey mustard—skip this and go for the exceptional smoky Blacktie Bourbon or vinegary tart Lowcountry Buffalo hot sauces), and these babies border on dangerously addictive. Fries are hand-cut and fried to order as well. Platters kindly include a cup of tangy slaw and a square of sweet cornbread. Still hungry? Finish it all off with Hubee's "Famous" fried banana pudding and bring friends, please! It's a deconstructed version of a Southern favorite, banana and 'Nilla pudding, this one showcasing a beignet-fried hot banana, real vanilla pudding, and a dusting of crumbled Nilla waters, hot chocolate, and caramel sauce. There is a limited selection of beer and wine at this very family-friendly spot. So friendly, Hubee's even offers all-you-can-eat salty, boiled peanuts to nosh during the short wait for supper.

The Med Bistro, 90 Folly Rd. at South Windermere Plaza, West Ashley, SC 29407; (843) 766-0323; www.themedbistro.com; Eclectic; $–$$. A restaurant destination of some sort for over 40 years, The Med Bistro's most recent incarnation is the best it's been in the past decade. Straightforward and unpretentious, The Med still feels a little bit special with a broad wine selection, a sophisticated beer mix, and cool, cosmopolitan looks. The food is, as the name implies, largely Mediterranean inspired in dishes like the sweet-potato ravioli with green peas, tomatoes, and sage, a lamb Bolognese over fettuccine and a crisp, refreshing poached-pear salad. A popular working folks' lunch spot, Med Bistro also serves some mean, generously portioned hungry-man dishes like a heaping Reuben or burger. Chunky, slightly piquant black bean soup is always on the menu. Parking is ample at this shopping center and it's just minutes from downtown.

Red Orchid's China Bistro, 1401 Sam Rittenberg Blvd., West Ashley, SC 29407; (843) 573-8787; www.redorchidsmenu.com; Chinese; $–$$. Dripping with paper lanterns and a sincere desire to please emanating from congenial husband-and-wife owners Tony and Kelly Chu, Red Orchid is hands-down the best Chinese restaurant in greater Charleston. It's a little tricky to find, tucked into a mall off of West Ashley's main drag, but it's well worth the effort. The soothing lettuce wraps filled with sizzling, savory chicken and silky shiitakes and the money-bag pork meatballs, wrapped in a crispy wonton with a spectacular ginger sauce, really bring home a taste-tingling payoff, while the house signature red snapper comes glazed with a hot/sweet sherry-and-cayenne glaze that will have you reaching for a cooling sip of sake. And, sake is something Tony Chu knows a lot about. Beyond a passion, he's a sake connoisseur who's been studying and tasting the stuff for years. The collection here is impressive and very fairly priced. Always impeccably clean and comfortable, you'll want to settle into the Red Orchid and stay awhile. Take-out is out of the question!

Zen Asian Fusion, 2037 Sam Rittenberg Blvd., West Ashley, SC 29407; (843) 766-6335; www.zenasianrestaurant.com; Asian Fusion/Sushi; $$. The cuisines of Thailand, China, Japan, Malaysia, and Indonesia are all lovingly represented in this pleasant melting "wok" handily situated near the merger of I-526 and Highway 17S in the heart of West Ashley. From the outside and the inside, it looks slightly Asian tacky, with glossy tables, lots of glass, and high-backed black booths. The kitsch is balanced with fountains and bamboo and, somehow agreeable, further amplified by the rock/techno music that sometimes plays a little bit too loudly. Always friendly and super clean, I love sneaking in here for a quiet lunch of tempura shrimp and vegetables and quite possibly one of the best ginger dressings I have ever had the pleasure to eat generously drizzled over ice-cold lettuce. Set lunch specials are exceptionally affordable and whether you opt for the Thai basil chicken or beef or the Chinese General Tso's chicken, you'll depart very satisfied, minus the guilt of blowing either your caloric or financial budgets. Zen hits the happy-karma mark best with its sushi, which is hand-rolled before all eyes to see at the handsome sushi bar that flanks the main dining room.

Al di La, 25 Magnolia Rd., West Ashley, SC 29407; (843) 571-2321; www.aldilarestaurant.com; Northern Italian; $$. During alfresco season, red Campari umbrellas dot the patio of this treasure trove of Northern Italian deliciousness tucked away in the Avondale neighborhood. The name Al di La translates from Italian to "celestial," and that's exactly what the food is here. Whether it's lunch, a drink and a small plate of the unforgettable braised *cipolline* or a wood-fired pizza at the Bacaro, a kind of Italian tapas bar, or a 4-course Italian extravaganza dinner, Al di La's food never disappoints. The fettuccine Bolognese, a creamy, chunky, and toothsome sauce cloaking fettucine that just yields to the bite, should get an award of some kind, a big one. Same goes for the signature ricotta and mascarpone gnocchi with shrimp, grape tomatoes, and basil. Fish preparations are consistently lovely, too. The setting is retro-Euro cosmopolitan and the Vespa that's usually parked out front makes you feel like tossing three coins in a Roman fountain. The wine list is relatively broad and fairly priced. There are two persistent, but not ever-present problems at Al di La, however. It can be very loud inside when it's busy, so consider visiting during off-peak hours. Also, while I've never had anything less than stellar to eat here, I have frequently (but not always) experienced service ranging from indifferent to flat-out rude, particularly at the hostess stand. Here's hoping you have better luck.

Gene's Haufbrau, 817 Savannah Hwy., West Ashley, SC 29407; (843) 225-4963; www.geneshaufbrau.com; Bar Food/Beer; $. For decades, this mustard and black colored bar has anchored Avondale with its special brand of stomach-lining bar grub and huge collection of domestic and imported ice-cold beer with over 150 varieties to choose from. Gene's is a veritable institution sporting all the classic bar fun and games, including darts, pool, shuffleboard, and even board games from Trivial Pursuit to Yahtzee. What may surprise you, however, is with all this going for it, Gene's throws in really good food too. Some of it, like the zesty portobello wrap and roasted red hummus, is healthy. But the best stuff, like the Southern-fried wings or loaded fries with melted cheddar, bacon, and scallions (with ranch dressing on the side for dipping!), is really bad for you, but tastes oh, so good going down.

The Glass Onion, 1219 Savannah Hwy., West Ashley, SC 29407; (843) 225-1717; www.ilovetheglassonion.com; Southern/Local; $–$$. The Glass Onion is so authentically Southern, you can practically hear a screen door creaking, see a firefly on a sultry summer night, and touch your mama's ruffled apron. Owned and operated by three young and talented chefs from different areas of the South, The Glass Onion (more commonly called The GO) peppers its menu with influences from the bayou, the Lowcountry, and the rural

South and seasons everything with the sweet, fresh kiss of utterly local, fresh, and largely organic produce, eggs, meat, and fish. Never fussy, the food (ordered from an ever-changing blackboard menu) sings with unfettered freshness in simple fare from deviled eggs to fried flounder over grits with braised greens. It's the kind of place that, once discovered, is never far from your heart and all but mandates multiple return visits. The creamy, silky pasta shells and cheese paired with the crisp and buttery Bibb lettuce salad dressed with the black-pepper buttermilk dressing is simply nirvana on a plate, or two. Sarah O'Kelley oversees all things sweet and regularly turns out old-fashioned wonders like peach pound cake with buttercream icing, homemade peppermint ice cream, and chocolate chip cookies that would make a grown man cry or at least fall in love! Tuesday night fried chicken suppers should be on everyone's bucket list—but don't forget reservations are required for this made-to-order Southern delight. Just about 10 minutes from downtown and with ample parking, The Glass Onion hits the delicious, down-home mark on every front, every time. That's why it's on my Best of Charleston Top Ten Must Do's list. Please put it on yours. See Sarah O'Kelley's recipe for **Red Velvet Pound Cake** on p. 220.

Middleton Place Restaurant, 4300 Ashley River Rd., West Ashley, SC 29414; (843) 266-7477; www.middletonplace.org; Lowcountry/Southern; $$–$$$. A lovelier, more pastoral and soulful setting is hardly imaginable. Grazing sheep, colonial architecture, and historic landscaped gardens just dripping with azaleas and camellias (depending on the season) form the backdrop at exquisite Middleton Place. The diminutive restaurant, situated in a former guest cottage, sits on the edge of all this loveliness, over-looking a rice mill pond and azalea hillside. It serves both lunch and dinner, but lunch here requires a day admission to the museum. After strolling through the gardens, lunch makes a well-suited finale to your visit. The menu borrows almost exclusively from the Lowcountry, sustainable recipe cards of former resident chef Edna Lewis and it is truly delicious. The Charleston she-crab soup is stunning with sherry, roe, and blue crab—just the way it was meant to be. Chase these with hot, crispy fried chicken livers with braised collards and redeye gravy, Lowcountry hoppin' John, and a sweet taste of divinity in a Huguenot torte with caramel sauce. Prices on the dinner menu creep a little bit higher, but so too, does the romance. Candlelit and cozy, the setting is serene and doesn't require museum admission fees to enter.

Old Firehouse Restaurant, 6350 Hwy. 162, Hollywood, SC 29449; (843) 889-9512; www.oldfirehouserestaurant.com; Southern/Eclectic; $-$$. If you find yourself about 30 minutes south of downtown with a rumbling belly, quiet it at this charming, brick former firehouse where big plates of classically homespun fare are the order of the day. Count the Dalmatian curios during your short and always pleasant wait for the likes of whole fried flounder with peach chutney, fried green tomatoes over creamy grits, or house-made pimento cheese with a sweet onion kick. The Old Firehouse smokes it out with fabulous wood-burning-oven pizzas, in particular the four cheese, which just oozes with mild cheeses cradled with a crunchy, lightly charred crust.

Po' Pigs Bo-B-Q, 2410 SC Hwy. 174, Edisto Island, SC 29438; (843) 869-9003; Barbecue; $. An actual white picket fence charmingly corrals hungry 'cue lovers to the buffet table at Po' Pigs, which is drenched with smoked pig and all the fixins—rice, turnip greens, lima beans, sweet potatoes, hush puppies, and more. The hash, a slightly sweet, deeply savory concoction prepared from pork parts is the real deal and especially delicious served over a mound of fragrant white rice. The restaurant, named after owner-chef Robert "Bo Bo" Lee, sits alongside a gas station on an otherwise lonely stretch of road on the edge of Edisto Island. Desserts and sweet tea are delicious here, but don't expect beer or wine. It's not served. The best "sauce" at Bo's comes in a bottle and tastes just right drizzled over the tender, naked smoked pork.

Specialty Stores, Markets & Producers

Avondale Wine & Cheese, 813-B Savannah Hwy., West Ashley, SC 29407; (843) 769-5444; Wine & Cheese. Wine and cheese aficionado

Manoli Davani rules the roost at this charming little red shop infused with the alluring scent of aged cheese and faint hint of red wine. Davani is passionate about both and personally cuts and serves more than 100 different cheeses and offers more than 200 wine choices. Step in and stay a while. There are comfortable tables and chairs for lingering in this tasty bubble of quiet away from the hustle and bustle of the modern world and Savannah Highway, which is just outside the front door.

Geechie Boy Market and Mill, 2995 S.C. Hwy. 174, Edisto Island, SC 29438; (843) 209-5220; www .geechieboymill.com; Stone ground grits and specialty shop. Come see the biggest red rocking chair and the largest portable corn mill—at a whopping 1,700 pounds—in action at this small store with big heart. Built on dreams and hard work, the mill is a testimony to owner Greg Johnsman's love of milling. The store sells bags of yellow and white ground cornmeal and grits, as well as fresh veggies, fresh bread, honey, jams, and more.

Johns Island, Kiawah Island & Wadmalaw Island

These beautiful barrier islands each represent the epitome of the Lowcountry's iconic scenic allure—they're all sea and sand and marsh dotted with towering pines and majestic live oaks dripping with Spanish moss. Kiawah Island, once remote farmland, is now home to a glittering resort, The Sanctuary, and many well-hidden, multimillion-dollar homes. Johns Island, and especially Wadmalaw, are much less developed, but sadly, that's changing with the winds of time and a growing population.

Enjoy them while you can! The drive through Johns Island and out to Kiawah is the cheapest and most enthralling vacation you'll ever take. Halfway there, the arch of live oaks and surprise peeks into sweeping marshes will have you utterly entranced. It's like instant meditation and wonder! Be careful, however, the road is narrow and winding and tightly hugged by the trees. It is dangerous and two lanes only. It is thus heavily patrolled and the fines are steep. The first time I fell under its stupor-inducing spell not long after I moved to Charleston, I made the mistake of driving (well) over the speed limit and got hit with a $250 doozy.

Foodie Faves

Fat Hen Restaurant, 3140 Maybank Hwy., Johns Island, SC 29455; (843) 559-9090; www.thefathen.com; French/Lowcountry; $$. Just a few miles down the road from **Wild Olive** (p. 149), this little red restaurant packs some serious, serious flavor punch. Credit goes to super-talented veteran chef-owner Fred Neuville. A devoted family man, he runs the restaurant with his wife Joan and stocks its larder with vegetables from his own farm, and eggs and chickens from his own chicken coop. Talk about backing up your restaurant's name! Easy and laid back, Fat Hen is also sophisticated. The menu showcases classic French bistro staples like steak frites, French onion soup, and escargots (all magnificent), but Neuville's main emphasis is integrating French technique with Lowcountry ingredients in daily specials and menu items like the tomato, roasted corn, and boiled peanut salad and a sweet, local flounder *niçoise*. The setting is as cute as the name; it looks a little like a farmhouse from the outside, complete with a screened-in porch, while inside it's full of rustic wood and friendly charm. There's even a little trail of chicken-feet imprints to lead you to the door. Sunday brunch is a super hot and popular commodity at the Fat Hen—you'll want to make reservations.

Jasmine Porch, 1 Sanctuary Beach Dr., Kiawah Island, SC 29455; (843) 768-6253; www.kiawahresort.com; Lowcountry/Southern; $$$. Serving breakfast, lunch, and dinner, Jasmine Porch offers one of the most soothing dining rooms you could ever hope to find. Sun spills in from huge windows that overlook the Atlantic and the resort's gorgeous swimming pool. Seats are deep and cozy and the living is easy supping on this restaurant's definitely Lowcountry fare. Whimsical pairings, such as the "Lunch on the Porch"—a plate of she-crab soup, fried chicken salad, and a crab cake, which seems filling enough but light enough for the spa set that frequents these tony parts. Treat yourself to the experience if you're out this way, the entire resort space is gorgeous. The Sunday jazz brunch is another big draw at the Jasmine Porch.

Stono Markets Tomato Shed Cafe, 842 Main Rd., Johns Island, SC 29455; (843) 559-9999; www.stonofarmmarket.com; Southern; $. What's not to love at Tomato Shed Cafe? As cute as a button, the owners have their own farm, Ambrose Family Farms, on Wadmalaw Island and bring the fresh goods here to be cooked up into a frenzy of homestyle Southern goodness. Oh, and there is a baker named Jeannie in the house who produces the flakiest biscuits and sweetest lemon chess pie around. Southern country classics like yellow squash casserole, tomato pie, butter beans, crab cakes, macaroni and cheese, and more tug at your heart strings and taste for nostalgia, even as they're served on your gingham cloth–lined table by a sweet, matronly type with a pencil behind her ear and a notepad in her hand. Truly delicious, Tomato Shed Cafe is situated on the edge of an actual market where you can shop for fresh eggs, vegetables, honey, and more or grab a prepared meal to bring home.

Wild Olive Cucina Italiana, 2867 Maybank Hwy., Johns Island, SC 29455; (843) 737-4177; www.wildoliverestaurant.com; Italian; $$. Situated pretty much halfway between downtown and the far end of Johns Island, getting to the Wild Olive is an easy trip whether you're coming from downtown or Kiawah. Because of this, and because of the fact that it is so darn good, Wild Olive is frequented heavily by locals and tourists or second-home owners during peak season. So be prepared for crowds (and lots of children) at these times and plan ahead. Executive chef Jacques Larson is perhaps Charleston's most unsung chef in terms of his raw talent and passion. The man is a genius and the food that comes out of his kitchen is consistently remarkable. Braised short ribs with a fontina-stuffed risotto cake and a pine-nut gremolata speak volumes about his talent and as succinctly as his simpler comfort foods like tomato-braised meatballs and lovely, cheesy lasagna. The setting is one of the smartest around, too. Pine shimmers with warm tones and contrasts beautifully with the rustic sophistication of captain's chairs and padded banquettes. A huge community table dominates the bar area of this white bungalow on the side of the road.

Landmarks

The Ocean Room, 1 Sanctuary Beach Dr., Kiawah Island, SC 29455; (843) 768-6253; www.kiawahresort.com; Steakhouse/ Seafood; $$$$. The only steakhouse in the United States to receive both Forbes Four-Star and AAA Four Diamond ratings, The Ocean Room prances through the high cotton of fine dining. The setting is sumptuous with gorgeous ironwork, an arch of windows looking over the sea and beach, and elegant woodwork. Executive Chef Nathan Thurston is 100% devoted to all things local, organic, seasonal, and in the case of beef, grass-fed. Dining here is an indulgence you'll pay handsomely for, but the taste rewards will be high. Chef Thurston knows how to have fun with his food in dishes that are almost playful while being profoundly delicious. Flounder dumplings with wild ramps, morel mushrooms, and a smoked ginger broth or seared diver scallops with pork belly, strawberry black-pepper jam and heirloom oats are just two examples. Jackets are preferred but not required. Reservations suggested. For lighter, less pricey dining, consider starting dinner a little bit earlier and selecting from the "Dinner at Dusk" menu.

Specialty Stores, Markets & Producers

Charleston Tea Plantation, 6617 Maybank Hwy., Wadmalaw Island, SC 29487; (843) 559-0383; www.charlestonteaplantation .com; Tea Plantation. America's only tea garden and home to American Classic Tea is situated on 127 verdant acres of open land that are truly a sight to see. The plantation offers trolley tours through the fields, an exclusive tour with owner Bill Hall, and perhaps the most interesting of all, a tour through the tea factory to watch tea leaves being processed and learn more about tea in general. Charleston Tea Plantation hosts a huge party every spring called the First Flush in honor of the first flush of tea leaves of the new growing season.

Firefly Distillery, www.fireflyvodka.com; Distillery. Jim Irvin (yes, of **Irvin House Vineyards,** below) and Scott Newitt were hanging out one hot, sultry South Carolina day dreaming of sweet tea and agreeing that the only thing that might make it better would be a little "kick." And, so Firefly Sweet Tea Vodka was born. From there, the distillery's product list has expanded to several different flavors, including Sweet Tea Bourbon. The stuff is potent and delicious. It's available for purchase (see terms) through the website and at many retail locations in greater Charleston and elsewhere.

Irvin House Vineyards, 6775 Bears Bluff Rd., Wadmalaw Island, SC 29487; (843) 559-6867; Winery. South Carolina's only vineyard is just 25 minutes of a beautiful drive into rural tranquility from downtown. Wine lovers will appreciate the experience and the wine. Tastings and tours of the scenic vineyards are available. Irvin House prepares five varieties of wine, all produced from the uniquely Southern Muscadine grape.

Slather Brand Foods, www.slatheriton.com; Specialty Sauce. Innovative entrepreneur, pistol of positive energy, and Johns Island resident Robin Rhea created a line of piquant/sweet sauces herself and is developing a huge following. What Rhea deems "The Cure for Boring Food," the original and spicy Slatherin' Sauce is just that. The sauce is a blend of pineapple, tomatoes, and more with a tantalizing blend of spices that makes it great with and cooked in just about anything. It's easily purchased online at the website listed above.

Savannah

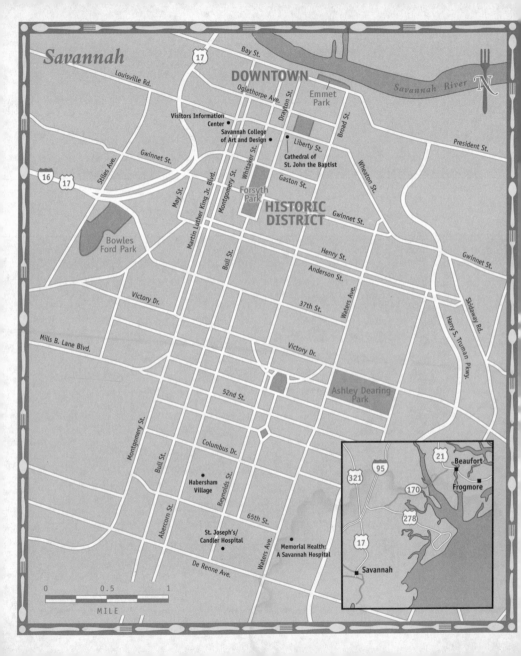

Introduction

Perhaps because of their proximity to one another (just 110 miles apart), people have spent centuries comparing Charleston and Savannah. Natives from either city can get especially hot-headed defending their particular piece of Lowcountry turf. Perhaps because I'm an identical twin and have listened to people compare my sister Heather and me for decades, I'm a little sensitive to the comparisons made between these two cities I know and love.

In my mind, it's perhaps more relevant to reflect upon their myriad similarities. First and foremost, both are situated in the heart of the Lowcountry, and thus share a similar larder from land and sea to develop their respective culinary styles. Both are port cities with big bridges, both were early American colonies (though Charleston was founded 40 years earlier), and, of course, both are dazzlingly beautiful (though their architecture and city designs are distinctly different).

Savannah was founded in 1733, by a brilliant, idealistic Utopian with a soft-spot for the poor and indebted souls of British society named James Edward Oglethorpe. He believed in hard work,

good behavior, and an even playing field for all members of society. Indeed, the early rules in Savannah prohibited a curious mix of ingredients: lawyers, rum, Papists (or Catholics, they were too closely aligned with the Spanish in nearby Florida), and, especially, slavery. His vision was complete and exceptionally methodical and is directly linked to Savannah's celebrated squares, which Oglethorpe personally designed to thrive as classless, independent, self-sufficient, mini-communities that were interwoven with the whole of the town through a series of streets and alleys. The structure of the city contributed to the construction of Savannah's many rows of town houses along her streets, which drip with Spanish moss that lends a kind of gentle grey mist to the entire place, softening all of her beautiful edges with distinctly Southern charm.

Oglethorpe's was a beautiful and expertly executed dream, but like most dreams, it, or at least most of his ideals, eventually drifted away with a growing tide of many complicated realities. In less than 4 decades from her founding date, lawyers (and lots of them), rum, Catholics, and slaves made their way into Savannah, along with an increasingly diverse pool of immigrants from Scotland, Ireland, Germany, Portugal, and elsewhere, many seeking religious asylum and a new life. Of these influences, it was arguably the introduction of the slaves' African culinary and social traditions that most affected what and how Savannahians ate, then and now. With them came increased rice production and rice consumption, which made their way into the gumbos and pirlous in Savannah's kitchens, and eventually restaurants, where they can all be deliciously sampled today.

Like the city itself, Savannah's culinary scene is decidedly more compact than Charleston's. Most of the restaurants I visited here on many delicious eating tours (what I came to call my nibble and scribble trips), were within the 1-mile radius that comprises most of downtown and the historic district. Not surprisingly, chefs and food artisans here are exploring the growing trend toward green and farm-to-table, local sourcing that celebrates seasonal, fresh cooking. There is a large arsenal of eateries and foodie haunts that are targeted to appeal to the massive number of Savannah College of Art and Design (better known as SCAD) students who roam the streets of Savannah in search of good, creative, and relatively cheap eats. Asian, French, South African, Spanish, and more are as evenly distributed as the tea rooms and Southern cuisine most usually equate with Savannah. If it's in this book, it means that it's worth a trip. There is something for every mood, every occasion, and every budget.

Take time to savor Savannah. She is a city that somehow weeps and seeps beauty, with a tiny touch of tragedy. Her tender soul is especially palpable at dawn and dusk, when her sleepy, relative silence beckons from her many bench-lined squares, exquisite fountains, and antique architecture. Sit back and listen to her stories and her people and her past, even as you experience her glorious, well-preserved present.

So, come along with me and let's savor Savannah!

Getting Around

Thanks to Mr. Oglethorpe's fine city planning, and Savannah's manageable size and outstanding management of parking and public transportation, getting around town is delightfully facile.

The parks are neatly arranged in rows moving from the Savannah River waterfront down to the south side of town toward the Victorian District and magnificent Forsyth Park. Each square represents a one-way kind of round-about driving opportunity and the longer, north and south running streets are easy to find and navigate.

Walking would be the transportation mode of choice for those who are able to stroll reasonable distances. It's really the best way to get to know and see Savannah, much as I recommend in Charleston. Each verdant square and every step of the way offers a plethora of viewing pleasures and it's extra easy to just stop and rest for a bite at one of the many restaurants and eateries downtown.

Because parking is so ample (more on that in a bit), driving is probably the second best choice. If your lodging or home is a good distance from downtown, as my home away from home, the Catherine Ward House, is, it might be best to drive the mile or so into town, park, and roam about downtown for the day. The restaurant-rich south side of town, which is home to **the Starland District** (see p. 190) and Habersham Village, represents an ambitious, multi-mile walk and is probably best traveled via a car or another form of transportation (see Alternative Modes of Transportation, below).

When driving, take your time and take notice, especially when navigating the squares. Moving vehicles are required to yield to oncoming traffic pouring into the squares from abutting streets. It's a little bit "blind" as you're turning the circle around the squares. Be sure to slow down, look to your right for oncoming traffic, and yield accordingly. Another note of caution has to do with pedestrians. As I've noticed they do in Charleston, people visiting a lovely city like Savannah tend to be distracted to the point of being dotty and are practically oblivious to moving vehicles, even when they're oncoming. And, to add insult to (possible) injury, in Savannah, pedestrians have the right of way when crossing streets, even if a green light suggests you do.

Street parking is abundant all over town with some "free" space, but mostly metered parking. There are several city lots throughout the city, most appointed with nifty little payment boxes equipped to read credit and debit cards, so cash is not required. Rates are very reasonable as well. If you do happen to get a parking ticket (as

I did—errh!—for a meter that expired while I was enjoying lunch), it's a relatively light hit compared to Charleston's $40 tickets in a similar space. On my unlucky parking day in Savannah, the damage was a mere $15!

Alternative Modes of Transportation

Chatham Area Transit (CAT), www.catchacat.org. The environmentally friendly lime and dark green public buses can be spotted all over town traversing their multiple networks of easily accessed stops and starts. Go to their website for routes and rates. Safe to use (though always pay extra attention after dark no matter where you are in a strange city) and clean, they're an easy and pleasant way to move around Savannah.

Motorini Vespa Savannah, 236 Drayton St., downtown Savannah, 31401; (912) 201-1899; www.vespa savannah.com. Flex your inner Italian and catch a breeze whisking down Savannah streets in true Euro style. This mode of transportation seems especially well-suited to Savannah and is a fun and reasonable way to move, if you're a brave, adventurous, open-air sort of guy or gal. It's legal to park these rented scooters on the sidewalks for an added free-parking bonus.

Old Town Trolley of Savannah, (912) 233-0083; www.trolley tours.com/savannah. An excellent way to familiarize yourself with the city is to take a versatile "hop on, hop off" tour on the Old Town Trolley. These charming green and orange trolleys whisk about town at 15 rotating stops and starts, including Mercer House (the scene of the crime in the popular book and movie filmed in Savannah, *Midnight in the Garden of Good and Evil,* simply referred to in Savannah as "the book") and restaurant and retail-rich Broughton Street. You can hop on and off to your heart's content throughout the day, learning from the driving guides' instructive monologues, and expect to pay somewhere between $20 and $25 when it's all said and done.

Keeping Up with Food News

Savannah Daily News, www.savdailynews.com. As the name implies, this is Savannah's online daily newspaper. Along with general news, it provides restaurant news and reviews, food columns and recipes, and more good stuff to satisfy foodie info cravings.

www.connectsavannah.com. Newsy and artsy, this is where to go to find out what's happening in "news, arts and entertainment for the coastal empire," as the motto goes. There is also good restaurant information here, too, for discerning foodies.

www.hellosavannah.com. This comprehensive and current site offers insights into all things Savannahian—what to do, where to do it, and where to find information about everything from restaurants to hotels. There is information on health, movies, pets and social networking, as well.

www.outside.in/savannah-ga/tags/restaurant. This link will bring you directly to the metro area dining section of this general Savannah information and news site.

www.visitsavannah.com. An Internet conduit of the CVB and Visitors Center, this well-designed, scenic, and informative site gives a little bit of information on a lot of Savannah highlights, from tours to restaurants. It's extra helpful for booking hotel reservations and planning activities as well as meals. The Visitor Center itself is located in a beautiful, historic old train depot at 301 Martin Luther King Jr. Blvd., Savannah, GA 31401; (912) 944-0455. It includes a museum, oodles of visitor information, and even a cafe in an antique railroad car.

Food Events

Forsyth Farmers' Market, south end (near the tennis courts), Forsyth Park, downtown Savannah; www.forsythfarmersmarket.org. For all of their loveliness, Oglethorpe's celebrated squares have nothing on this sprawling park in the Victorian District heading toward the south side of town. Its entire perimeter is rimmed with live oaks dripping with Spanish moss and it boasts a stunning, white Victorian fountain at the entrance. Busy from day until night with runners, walkers, picnics, and frivolity, in many ways Forsyth Park is the heart of Savannah. Between 9 a.m. and 1 p.m. on Saturday from April through November, the Savannah Local Food Collaborative hosts the Forsyth Farmers' Market and "Food for All." Honey, mushrooms, shrimp, herbs from Mary Curly the Herb Lady, and potent, locally roasted Perc coffee can all be found here along with the sense of convivial community only farmers' markets can deliver. There is even a Health Pavilion where kids (and adults) can learn more about healthy eating and lifestyles.

Savannah Craft Brew Fest, www.savannahcraftbrewfest.com. Savannah's annual celebration of craft brews takes place near or around Labor Day during this 3-day festival that includes an elegant beer- and wine-pairing dinner, a grand tasting event of over 120 craft brews overlooking historic Savannah and the Savannah River by the waterfront, and an awards celebration for the best brew.

Savannah Restaurant Week, www.savannahrestaurantweek.net. A celebration of delicious dining on the relative cheap, Savannah's

Restaurant "Week" actually lasts a full 10 days. A number of restaurants have participated in the past, and the group just keeps getting bigger and better. From late January through early February, participating restaurants offer special 3-course menus for $30. It's simple enough! Just make your reservation and when you get there, tell them you're participating in Restaurant Week to get the special menu and pricing.

The Best of Savannah—Top Ten Must-Do's

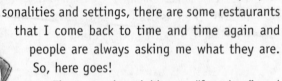

I find it difficult to pick favorites, mostly because mine change with my mood and with what I'm craving on any particular day. Yet because of their consistent deliciousness and unique personalities and settings, there are some restaurants that I come back to time and time again and people are always asking me what they are. So, here goes!

These are invariably my "favorites" and I think they'll be yours, too. This list doesn't exclude the deliciousness of all the other restaurants/eateries listed in this book, but these stand out for their excellence. They are all situated in or near downtown Savannah.

Savannah, Downtown/ Historic District

Oh, beautiful downtown Savannah! She really "begins" at the Savannah River and River Street and keeps moving south to 37th Street, flanked by Martin Luther King Jr. Boulevard and East Broad at the west and east, respectively. It is here where you'll find the greatest concentration of historic architecture and eateries, most of which can be travelled by foot. This is the "downtown" I think of when I think of Savannah, and I think most visitors feel the same way. Beyond 37th, there are definitely neighborhoods (particularly Habersham Village and the Starland District) that are up and coming, hip, foodie targets where "green" and homespun and exotic all commingle in her culinary melting pot. Because they're relatively small, I'm leaving them under the "downtown" heading, but will list their complete addresses so you will have no problem finding your way there.

Savannah's pace is unrushed and easy, and this translates to the way food is prepared and consumed here, whether lingering over the amazing fried chicken and platters of mashed potatoes and gravy at **Mrs. Wilkes' Dining Room** (p. 196) or in the Euro-centric, locavore cool of **Local 11 Ten** on Bull (p. 182). There is so much to enjoy as you make your way through town. Bon appétit, y'all!

Foodie Faves

Alligator Soul, 114 Barnard St., downtown Savannah, GA 31401; (912) 232-7899; www.alligatorsoul.com; Southern/Cajun; $$$. Located in the basement of a former grain warehouse (circa 1885) off of historic Telfair Square, Alligator Soul gives off a romantic, clandestine glow. The old, timeworn brick walls give the setting a soft embrace that's set off by gorgeous woodwork behind the bar, dim lighting, and beautiful artwork. A cluster of sofas sits comfortably off in a corner in front of an inviting fireplace. The best way to begin a meal here is with the stunningly simple and delicious artisan cheese plate that showcases a rotating selection of nutty, fragrant, locally produced cheeses, toasted whole walnuts, and a generous chunk of sweet, oozing **Savannah Bee Company** (see p. 204) honeycomb. With fruit, it's a light meal in itself. But don't stop there, the Creole-infused shrimp and grits rock with a touch of heat and tasso, tempered perfectly with a swirl of soothing, milky cheddar. Cajun and Creole staples like andouille, dark roux, and the mirepoix trinity of celery, onion, and green peppers, show up a lot here in many dishes that are slightly overcharged with flavors and ingredients. The end result, largely due to the setting and pleasant service staff, is a pleasant one, but the flavors in some of the dishes sometimes seem a little confused. Focus on what looks simplest, and you'll find Alligator's truest and tastiest soul.

Al Salam Deli, 2311 Habersham St. (at 40th), downtown Savannah, GA 31401; (912) 447-0400; Middle Eastern; $. As if to remind you that there is a world outside of Savannah and Southern food, the walls at this tiny deli with huge heart are lined with covers of old National Geographic magazine covers. The husband-and-wife owners work the counter like clockwork. She takes the orders, he does the cooking, and it all works like a charm. The baba ghanoush is rife with lemon and garlic, smooth as pudding, and even better with ultrafresh pita wedges dipped into its silky goodness. Lamb gyros and falafel rule here, as surely as the sun sets every evening and rises every day. Al Salam's an eat-in, or take-out kind of place with lots of regulars and a truly feel-good neighborhood vibe. Call ahead if you want to skip a wait in line. While you're there, check out the interesting assortment of imported candies and groceries to fill your at-home pantry.

Angel's BBQ, 21 W. Oglethorpe Ln., downtown Savannah, GA 31401; (912) 495-0902; www.angels-bbq.com; Barbecue; $. Crazy, cluttered kitsch, from green St. Patrick's Day beads to colorful hot-pepper lights, adorns this tiny, mildly hole-in-the-wall 'cue joint. It's tough to find on little-traveled Oglethorpe Lane (near Bull Street), but make the effort. Next to Blowin' Smoke, this is the best pig in Savannah. Angel's barbecue comes from the shoulder, or "butt," of the pig dressed in a perky and traditional Georgia Lowcountry tomato and cider vinegar–based sauce. Angel's Special is a pulled-pork sandwich with coleslaw, tossed in a sweet yellow mustard sauce that is tangy and gorgeous with the mild, round, and smoky flavors of the pork. There is limited seating and some of it is outside under spacious umbrellas.

Back in the Day Bakery, 2403 Bull St., Savannah (Starland District), GA 31401; (912) 495-9292; Bakery/Cafe; $. At first thought, sweet is the best word that comes to mind to describe this endearing, pink and ruffled retro bakery in the heart of the Starland District. A husband-and-wife team, Griffith and Cheryl Day do all the baking and cooking here from scratch, every day. And that's where the second best word to describe Back in the Day comes to mind: savory. Griffith is the mastermind behind savory tarts and quiches and creates the bakery's signature ciabatta, which is made daily and envelops fat, tasty sandwiches, like a bacon and onion jam sandwich or a butterbean hummus sandwich stacked with crunchy cukes, carrots,

red onion, sharp cheddar cheese, tomato, and lettuce. He does amazing soups, too. Cheryl's pastry confections are as beautiful to look at as they are to eat. Red velvet cupcakes, banana cream pie, drunk blondies, bourbon bread pudding and much, much more will disarm you with their looks, but they'll seduce you with their tantalizing taste and texture. No matter what your fancy, including a steaming, rich cup of espresso, Back in the Day can satisfy it, in a big, delicious way. That's why Back in the Day is on the Top Ten Must Do's Savannah list. Do it!

Bar Food, 4523 Habersham St., Habersham Shopping Village, just south of downtown Savannah, GA 31405; (912) 355-5956; www.bar foodsavannah.com; Tapas/Eclectic; $–$$. I visited this most aptly named hot spot in the Habersham Shopping Village south of historic Savannah on a Tuesday night. That's a good thing or a bad thing, depending on how you look at it. Tuesday is $1 drink special night. The night I was there, the special was a fruity, fabulous sangria, and the crowds were out in force. So much so that it was difficult to find a seat in the small, energetic bar, which happens to serve some very good food. Lacking a full and functional kitchen, they manage to send out some wonderful stuff, in particular the steamed dumplings, which come in a bamboo steamer with a sweet/hot soy-ginger dipping sauce. Try the Southern pupu platter for whimsical, international cross-breeding of goodness, or for just plain old Southern fun, a simple tomato sandwich. The crowd here is very colorful, very neighborhood friendly, and very Savannahian to say the least.

Blowin' Smoke BBQ, 514 MLK Jr. Blvd., downtown Savannah, GA 31401; (912) 231-2385; www.blowinsmokebbq.com; Barbecue; $-$$. Pig at Blowin' Smoke is smoked long and slow over fragrant Georgia pecan wood and is eventually bathed in a signature sauce of similarly smoked tomatoes, garlic, onions, and jalapeños that get a flavor finish with ketchup and vinegar. This is some delicious 'cue, no matter how you cut it: Ribs, loin, brisket, butt—all the big pig players are here! The hand-pulled pork sandwich is irresistible, especially when paired with a side of the fried pickles, which are coated in a lip-smacking lemon and pepper breading, much like the winning onion rings. The mood is casual and hip here, especially in the large, outdoor garden where Blowin' Smoke's extensive craft beer list pairs happily with a plate of pig.

Brasserie 529, 529 E. Liberty St., downtown Savannah, GA 34101; (912) 238-0045; www.brasserie529.com, French Brasserie; $$-$$$. With an easy, breezy mood and casual sophisticated setting, Brasserie 529 does a great job of re-creating French brasserie classics with a slightly modern edge. For example, a refreshing lobster and cucumber vol-au-vent served with a fragrant, crunchy celery leaf and fresh mint garnish and a grilled *salade niçoise* with a Merlot vinaigrette. But, Old-World staples like onion soup gratinée and fat, sweet, and tender wine-steamed mussels prevail here, along with a truly relaxed neighborhood setting and a convenient and ample parking lot. Prices can soar into the high zone with certain evening menu items, but for the most part Brasserie 529 is reasonable and serves reliable, consistent, and good food to be savored with friends and a craft beer or cool glass of imported French wine. Bon appétit!

Butterhead Greens Cafe, 1813 Bull St., Savannah (Starland District), GA 31401; (912) 201-1808; Sandwiches/Salads/Coffee; $. Located in the heart of the Starland District, directly across from a heavily student-trafficked SCAD building, Butterhead is devoted to all things fresh, simple, and unprocessed.

A huge, glass container of refreshing cucumber water anoints the beverage counter and a limited menu of refreshing sandwiches and sides keeps things simple. However, everything sounds and looks so amazing it's really tough making choices at Butterhead. If pressed, and not very hard, I'd go for the "Flightless Heaven" sandwich, a dreamy, layered delight of mesquite-smoked turkey, marinated red onion, oven-dried tomatoes and a house-made sage sauce. The quinoa salad is a nutty, chewy ode to the tasty grain, tossed with a Mediterranean mélange of red onions, tomatoes, lemon juice, olive oil, and oodles of herbs. Butterhead's not fancy, but it's very good if you're in the mood for some original, vegetable-oriented food choices. They also serve deep, rich, locally roasted Perc house blend coffee.

Cafe 37, 205 E. 37th St., Savannah (Starland District), GA 31401; (912) 236-8533; www.cafe37.com; Eclectic $$–$$$. It's a little tricky to spot this butter-yellow, wood-sided building, but it's worth the effort to do so. The perfect business, vacation, or ladies-who-lunch setting, the cafe serves breakfast, lunch, and dinner, moving further away from traditional Southern/American offerings as the hours move along, picking up French, Asian, and other international menu cues (as well as higher prices) as day becomes night. Executive Chef-Owner Blake Elsinghorst trained at Le Cordon Bleu in Paris and his classical acumen shines equally well in his silky Duck Liver Mousse with Cherry Gastrique as it does in a deliciously crisp fried oyster po' boy served with a creamy, chunky remoulade. The wedge salad, an ice-cold wedge of fresh iceberg, topped with an exceptional buttermilk dressing, crumbled fresh bacon, garden-fresh tomatoes, Roquefort and cucumber is one of the best versions I've had anywhere. On Thursday night, Cafe 37 becomes a popular tapas destination for bites of the likes of escargots and sautéed mussels and *foie gras* served in a white wine and truffle sauce. Can you say *oui*? There is a large and easily accessed parking lot to add to Cafe 37's eminent allure. See Blake Elsinghorst's recipe for **Duck Liver Mousse with Cherry Gastrique** on p. 226.

Cha Bella, 102 E. Broad St., downtown Savannah, GA 31401; (912) 790-7888; www.cha-bella.com; Organic/Eclectic; $$$. Everything at Cha Bella, from the large, somehow elegant chalkboard that announces the fresh picks from the garden and specials that day to the squeaky-clean, uncluttered menu, screams "fresh"! Executive

Chef-Owner Matthew Roher is vigilantly committed to getting the freshest, most local goods not just to his restaurant's table but also in his "Farm Box," CSA-style deliveries and in growing fresh, organically raised produce at his nearby farm, Avondale Farm. The farm sustains the larder for his catering company, Earth to Table. His commitment to all things fresh and sustainable shines in Cha Bella's radiant menu of minimalist preparations infused with loving and precise technique in dishes like white shrimp ("the world's most perfect," according to the menu) in light lemon Chardonnay and tarragon butter sauce or a small plate of Sapelo clams and house-made sausage in a roasted tomato, garlic, white-wine butter sauce. Something as simple as a steamed, seasonal, garden-fresh carrot tossed in house-made pasta and a gentle, buttery sauce can make you smile with its seductive and tasty simplicity. The restaurant looks rustic with chunky, farmhouse tables and elegant all at once, with sophisticated chandeliers and floor-to-ceiling taupe curtains. One of Savannah's best restaurants, it's also one of my top ten favorites (see p. 164). Tours are offered of Avondale Farm, which is just a few miles away. For more information, visit the restaurant's website posted above.

Circa 1875 Gastro Pub, 48 Whitaker St., downtown Savannah, GA 31401; (912) 443-1875; www.circa1875.com; French Bistro; $$–$$$. Circa 1875, located down near the river in the heart of the historic district, is a beautiful, old brick building that artfully combines a French pub and bistro mood with Southern colonial elegance. The gorgeous space is resplendent with French, feminine touches like delicate chandeliers and fluffy, white cloud paintings, and then brought gently down to earth with casual linen and brown-paper-lined tables. Whether you sit in the pub or in the more elegant dining room, you can expect to savor French bistro staples like steak tartare, hamburger au poivre, and a particularly bright and delicious version of a frisée salad, gently enveloped with a perky, tart/sweet cider and Dijon mustard dressing—fabulous! An extensive wine selection and specialty martinis fill out the libations list, which also includes several craft beers and European imports such as Stella Artois.

Clary's Cafe, 404 Abercorn St., downtown Savannah, GA 31401; (912) 233-0402; Breakfast/Lunch Cafe; $. Sometimes it seems like real-deal corned-beef hash has gone the way of dinosaurs and phone booths. It's just that hard to find. But it's served all day, every day at Clary's, a classic Old-World cafe that has been in operation since 1903. The hash is truly smashing, a chunky mélange of slow-cooked beef brisket, pulled, chopped, and tossed with tiny chunks of potatoes and grilled off to crispy-crunchy perfection. The menu makes several nods to old Jewish deli favorites including cheese blintzes, hoppel poppel (scrambled eggs with Kosher salami, potatoes, and green peppers), and hand-carved Norwegian smoked salmon served with bagels,

cream cheese, and all the fixings. The place has a definitive Aunt Bee feel to it, with slightly tattered and sticky tablecloths, paper order pads, and aprons aplenty. It's a classic old Savannah haunt and definitely worth the trip for a stick-to-your-ribs breakfast or lunch event. There is a second, newer location located at 4430 Habersham St. a little further south of town; (912) 351-0302.

FORM, 1801 Habersham St., historic Savannah, GA 31401; (912) 236-7642; www.form-cwg .com; Tastery/Wine Shop; $–$$. Ninety-five years of combined food and beverage experience among four very talented food and wine professionals reap delicious and varied rewards at this unique "tastery" near Forsyth Park. It is the perfect place to load up for a memorable picnic, beginning with a vat of the poppy-seed chicken salad which pops with sweet, purple grapes and butter-tender *sous-vide* cooked white chicken. Chase that with a cool glass of hand-picked, reasonably priced rosé from FORM's fine wine selection, grab a fresh baguette, and then, la crème de la crème, a wedge of co-owner Brian Torres' celestial cheesecake. The Brooklyn native started making it in his mother's kitchen at age 5, and he hasn't stopped perfecting cheesecake. One of his many tricks is to beat the filling for "hours"—it's simultaneously light and dense with a mild aftertaste reminiscent of caramel that resides somewhere in the crust. This may very well be one of the best cheesecakes on the planet. FORM also sells many locally made artisanal charcuterie and meat products and has a nice selection of hand-cut imported cheeses.

Gallery Espresso, 234 Bull St., downtown Savannah, GA 31401; (912) 233-5348; www.galleryespresso.com; Cafe; $. Officially the oldest coffee house in all of Savannah, Gallery Espresso is also one of the best. Coffee of all varieties is whipped up in a high-end Simonelli coffee machine, its whir and foam sounds and fragrant aromas infusing this corner spot with a sense of coziness that wafts through the equally cozy room full of eclectic chairs, small tables, sofas, and soft, deep armchairs. The setting makes it a great spot to people watch, or for the more focused, read or work on your computer at this free Wi-Fi location. Wine, beer, and other adult beverages nicely round out a long espresso and coffee list to complement the sophisticated menu of cheese plates, scones, Greek specialties, pies, cakes, tarts, and gluten-free desserts. Getting service at the counter can be slow when it's busy, which is a lot of the time.

Goose Feathers, 39 Barnard St., downtown Savannah, GA 34101; (912) 233-4683; www.GooseFeathersCafe.com; Breakfast/Sandwiches/Salads; $. There is nothing random, or duck, duck goose-like about choosing to stop at Goose Feathers. The heart and soul-warming food and cheerful red-and-white color scheme and goose theme make it an almost mandatory destination for big, gutsy breakfasts, pastries, bagels, and sandwiches, depending on the time of day and your mood. If the kid in you is out to play, sink your teeth into the soft, cakey whoopie pies with a creamy, indulgent filling. They come in all flavors, but the chocolate is especially decadent. Breakfast is big and satisfying, with thick Belgian waffles topped with whipped cream, bananas, pecans, and more, or cheesy, fluffy scrambled eggs tucked into fresh croissants. Pastry calling your name? Go with the gooey, delicious sticky buns or filled sweet croissants. Lunch is a bit more figure-friendly with lighter options including the sensational curried rice and edamame salad or a cool bowl of chunky gazpacho. Ample seating is available outside when weather allows, overlooking the leafy edges of lovely Ellis Square.

Green Truck Neighborhood Pub, 2430 Habersham St., Savannah (Starland District), GA 31401; (912) 234-5885; www .greentruckpub.com; Burgers/Soups/Salads; $. This neat grass-fed burger and craft-brew joint is a gem of a find on the outer edges of the green and hip **Starland District** (see sidebar, p. 190). Situated in what looks like a former fast-food stop (there are still remnants of an old drive-up window), Green Truck is all about slow food, made with love, and prepared from scratch using vigilantly sourced local producers and farmers. The beefy, boisterous burgers deliver with sweet, herbed, grass-fed beef flavor and come stacked with fresh veggies, cheeses, and a slew of house-made condiments

including pickles, ketchup, and a winning, creamy ranch dressing. Goat cheese, balsamic caramelized onions, roasted red peppers, and fresh basil dress the fabulous Rustico burger. There are also garden-fresh, crunchy salads so delicious, "They make cows jealous," as Green Truck's motto

states. If beef is not on your list, dig into the creamy, pungent house-made (of course!) pimento cheese sandwich and add bacon for $1 extra. The pub teems with an energetic and eclectic lunch crowd bellying up to booths and tables in everything from neckties to stained painter's overalls. Hot, made-to-order fries dipped in cool, sweet, tomato-fresh ketchup are extra delicious with one of Green Truck's rotating 30-something beer and brew choices. Their **Spiced Georgia Nuts** (see recipe on p. 225) are crunchy, delicious, and highly addictive!

The Gryphon Tea Room, 337 Bull St., downtown Savannah, GA 31401; (912) 525-5880; High Tea/Sandwiches; $–$$. Located in a magnificent circa-1913 building right on the corner of exquisite Madison Square, The Gryphon leaves many beautiful and mildly mysterious clues to its former long life as Solomon Pharmacy. It begins with the name "Solomon" built into the mosaic tiles at the entrance and continues with a border of 14 mortars and pestles depicted in Tiffany-style glass panels above the tea and coffee bar. There is even a series of drawers and cupboards that used to house the drugs at the apothecary. History aside, the space was recently renovated and currently shines with style and grace. The fabric-covered ceilings and cool, green-velvet floor-to-ceiling drapes help keep things quiet. The Gryphon serves assorted teas throughout the day, but the high tea from 4 to 6 p.m. is the consummate indulgence, with clotted cream, scones, and tea sandwiches. A simple lunch is lovely here, too. The menu is brief but delicious and includes a trio of scones—country ham and apple on a cheese scone, turkey and chow chow on a caraway-dill scone, and shrimp salad and watercress on a plain scone—as well as many stellar sandwiches and salads. Bring your patience to The Gryphon. Service from the largely SCAD student staff leans toward the slow side. Fortunately, the space is so exquisite it's the kind of place that invites lingering.

Harris Baking Company, 105 E. Liberty St., #101, downtown Savannah, GA 31401; (912) 233-6400; www.harrisbakingco.com; Bakery/Sandwiches/Soup; $. Located on the ground level of the Drayton Tower, one of Savannah's tallest buildings, this family-run bread, pastry, soup, and sandwich shop is a friendly and happy destination. Servers double as bakers and cooks, serving up smiles and giggles along with super-sticky sticky buns and gargantuan cinnamon rolls. The small, inviting space is fragrant with the smells of cinnamon and baking bread, but also does a wonderful job with the likes of a chunky lobster, shrimp, and crab bisque and savory tarts, especially the peppered bacon, cheddar, and caramelized onion tart. Retro black-and-white photography and metal chairs with pretty, comfortable French blue booths combine to make a nice setting to have lunch or breakfast.

Jazz'd Tapas Bar, 52 Barnard St., downtown Savannah, GA 31401; (912) 236-7777; www.jazzdsavannah.com; Southern-Style Tapas; $$. Toe-tappin', good tapas fun is on tap at this cosmopolitan, musical hot spot near Ellis Square. Live music, including jazz, swing, and even tunes from Savannah-born lyricist Johnny Mercer, plays on here 6 nights a week. Snazzy, sexy up-lighting on the serpentine bar makes for a perfect perch to indulge in a cool cocktail and some of the fabulous small plates coming out of Executive Chef Brian Gonet's kitchen. While most of the food is Southern or Lowcountry inspired, such as the chunky, creamy she-crab stew or the hot, fried, light-as-air shrimp fritters, others draw from international pantries, such as the fire-hot chorizo empanadas and the knock-out chicken lettuce wraps with peanut curry sauce, which has a pan-Asian flavor bent. These wraps pronounce themselves with serious spice, a touch of sweetness and plenty of fresh vegetable crunch. See Brian Gonet's recipe for **Chicken Lettuce Wrap with Peanut Curry Sauce** on p. 228.

Leoci's Trattoria, 606 Abercorn St., downtown Savannah, GA 31401; (912) 335-7027; www.leocis.com; Northern Italian; $$–$$$. Leoci's looks a little forlorn on this somewhat lonely block of Abercorn, not far from Forsyth Park and sitting across from a rundown-looking building. But inside, Leoci's is anything but forlorn. It's warm with authentic Italian conviviality, the glow of a woodburning brick oven, and the promise of authentic Italian fare from veteran chef and Italian native, Roberto Leoci. Mirrors and paintings give it an Old-World, sophisticated yet casual feel, and there is an expansive outdoor deck for alfresco dining when moods and weather cooperate. Almost all of the pasta is made in house and that's where Leoci's really shines, particularly with the clouds of lobster ravioli, stuffed with sweet chunks of fresh lobster robed with a rich, yet light, buttery champagne lobster sauce. Pizza comes with a lot of smoke flavor and a delightful crust; the simple *quattro formaggi,* topped with mozzarella, Parmesan, gorgonzola, and ricotta cheeses, is one of the best. An excellent choice for a quiet, romantic, or business lunch or dinner, or a festive night with friends on the patio, Leoci's also has relatively easy nearby on-street parking options.

Local 11 Ten, 1110 Bull St., downtown Savannah, GA 31401; (912) 790-9000; www.local11ten.com; Southern/Eclectic; $$$. Situated on the southern border of beautiful Forsyth Park, this delicious, local tidbit makes itself home in a 1950s-era former bank. The decor takes its cues from retro-land, with chunky, padded walls, and a cream, chocolate, and black color scheme. But the funky, Euro-beat music thumping near the bar and the food cues are thoroughly modern. Executive Chef Brandy Williamson wields some serious talent, infusing her classically French-themed dishes with huge, locally sourced, indigenous seafood and produce. The Cordon Bleu–trained chef gets high marks for ingenuity and clarity in everything that comes out of her kitchen, beginning with stellar, salt-crusted, warm rosemary bread that comes to the table served on a rustic wooden plank. "Prime meats and seafood" like a cowboy rib eye or wild Georgia shrimp are paired with your sauce of choice, including a knock 'em dead authentic, long-cooked and reduced demi-glace or decadent *foie gras* butter. Sides can be served a la carte, but it's the seasonal menu's paired entrees that ultimately showcase the talent here. Ponder the beautiful pairing of flavor and texture in the coriander-encrusted sea scallops with red beet puree, pearl onions, field beans, carrots, peppers, tendrils, and lemongrass butter. It sounds and tastes fresh as a garden, like most everything at this stand-out Savannah find, which is why it takes its place firmly on my Top Ten Must-Do's whilst visiting the Hostess City.

Lulu's Chocolate Bar, 42 MLK Jr. Blvd., downtown Savannah, GA 31401; (912) 238-2012 or toll-free (866) 461-8681; www.lulus chocolatebar.net; Desserts/Cocktails; $–$$. Sexy, sassy, and sweet, Lulu's is all about old-fashioned, girly, retro fun. Oh, and guys like it, too. The menu is streamlined and straightforward—saucy, chocolatey cocktails and an eye-popping arsenal of house-made desserts. It all comes your way via frilly, retro apron–clad servers and in the old, brick-walled confines of a petite building on MLK between Broughton and Congress Streets. Jamming tunes crank from a jukebox to keep things light while sipping on the likes of a Milky Way Martini or Raspberry Truffle Martini and nibbling on a slice of moist, decadent Strawberry Suspended Layer Cake or chewy, crunchy Caramel Tart. Lulu's is the perfect

après-dinner stop for a dash of sweet and a ton of cosmopolitan fun before you call it a night. You can enjoy a little bit of Lulu's at home with a **Savannah Bourbon Bellini** (see recipe on p. 224).

Noble Fare, 321 Jefferson St., downtown Savannah, GA 31401; (912) 443-3210; www.noblefare.com; Eclectic/Continental; $$$. Just thinking about Noble Fare is a feel-good opportunity. It's very much a friendly, family-run affair that began when husband-and-wife team Jenny and Patrick McNamara met and fell in love first with food and wine and then with each other. In 2007, they opened the restaurant inspired by their respective Gaelic names Patrick ("noble") and Jenny ("fair"). The beautiful brick house on Jefferson Street is both elegant and relaxed. Expect to be greeted by the lovely Jenny with the couple's infant Liv Ann usually in tow. Chef McNamara's food is highly original and, appropriately, he flaunts his flair for playful names in dishes like Duck-Duck-Duck-No Goose and Chocolate Love Cake, served with a silky custard ice cream and raspberry sauce. The food is to be taken seriously here, however. It's truly fabulous, and thus makes the Savannah Top Ten Must-Do list. Practically still moving they are so fresh, scallops seared to a crispy, caramel brown to showcase a milky, creamy sweet center are paired with a "risotto" that's actually prepared with sweet, fresh corn, bacon, and a sweet balsamic reduction in one of the chef's more noteworthy dishes. Noble Fare is the kind of place where details and friendliness matter. There is an in-house bakery upstairs that produces lovely fresh bread that is served with a variety of condiments including whipped butter, olive oil, 20-year aged vinegar, and pistachio-mint pesto. Dig in and enjoy! See Patrick McNamara's recipe for **Pan-Roasted Diver Scallops with Bacon & Corn Risotto** on p. 222.

Papillote, 218 W. Broughton St., downtown Savannah, GA 31401; (912) 232-1881; www.papillote-savannah.com; French Pastries & Sandwiches; $. Gaelic charm all but oozes from this delightful little spot situated just a few steps from the equally charming Paris Market shop. Ooh la la–worthy lavender *macarons* glitter in glass cases, just begging for a bite of their crisp, chewy goodness. Chef-Co-owner Herve Didailler hails from the Brittany region of France and he brings all that good French stuff home to roost at Papillote. A huge blackboard posts a list of fruity, refreshing libations, while the kitchen turns out one mean *croque monsieur,* with thick, toasted slices of ultrafresh, toasted bread enveloping a gooey béchamel, swiss cheese, crème fraîche, and sweet, salty ham. Petite, round bistro tables provide the perfect setting to dig into Papillote's *bouchée à la reine,* a kind of sophisticated potpie where the sauce is béchamel and the pastry is puff, or any one of the many tempting daily specials. The air tinkles with French accents that practically make you want to dance, or at least sing, "Non, je ne regrette rien" à la Edith Piaf. For these reasons and more, Papillote makes my Top 10 Must Do's list for Savannah. If you don't want to eat in, Papillote will wrap any and everything up most neatly for you to take home or to a garden bench for open-air dining, French style.

Rocks on the Roof, Bohemian Hotel, 102 W. Bay St., downtown Savannah, GA 34101; (912) 721-3800; www.bohemianhotelsavannah .com; Tapas/Bar Food; $$. "Rocks" is the cool place to be to beat Savannah's sultry heat and take in her sultry riverfront views. The beautiful food matches the panoramic vistas. A wood-fired grill and fire pit set the stage for a relaxed, cosmopolitan setting for consuming fragrant Parmesan truffle fries or lovely chicken and waffle sliders with Boursin cheese and plucky pepper jam. Oyster sliders are neat with a refreshing cocktail and easy bar banter or try the Tuscan beef bruschetta dancing with the pungency of blue cheese and the sweetness of balsamic vinegar. Martinis are ultraclean tasting and prepared with organic vodka. The Cool as a Cucumber Martini is infused with the gentle, crisp flavor of real cucumbers and is as refreshing as a cool breeze on a hot summer's day. Dress your best and polish your shoes. This is a place to turn a few heads and to see and be seen during a night out on Savannah town.

Sammy Green's, 1710 Abercorn St. (between 33rd and 34th Streets), downtown Savannah, GA 34101; (912) 232-1951; www .sammygreens.com; Sliders/Hot Dogs; $. A bright yellow-and-green awning at the corner of 34th and Abercorn lets you know you've arrived at this sunny little spot with huge slider and hot dog flavor. The young trio that owns and operates Sammy's is from the northeast and the flavor-packed food that they serve here (sweet tea aside) is highly reminiscent of the street food that you can find all over Manhattan. Except it is better. The setting is cool and casual and you can sit down for a spell while you eat. Orders are taken at the counter, quickly fulfilled, and delivered with a smile. That's when the real fun begins, especially if you ordered any of the slow-roasted beef-brisket sliders which are absolutely tender, slightly fatty, moist bites of heaven on cute little lightly toasted soft buns. At just $2.50 a pop, they're budget friendly and bursting with flavor. The mellow beef is paired with crunchy shredded cabbage, fresh onion, cucumber, a creamy *tzatziki* sauce and a spicy *sriracha* in the *doner* slider while the Chee Booger is all-American, smothered with gooey yellow cheese over onions, pickle chips, yellow mustard, and a *tschirky* sauce for good foreign measure. If beef is not your thing, dig into the slow-roasted pulled-pork shoulder or chicken breast cutlet sliders (also don't forget the dogs!), which all showcase equally inventive and delicious sauces and toppings.

Sapphire Grill, 110 W. Congress St., downtown Savannah, GA 31401; (912) 443-9962; www.sapphiregrill.com; Southern/Eclectic; $$$. Though he employs some Southern and Lowcountry influences in his dynamic "fresh market cuisine," Chef-Proprietor Christopher Nason in many ways tours the globe for more remote regional inspirations, even while he tours the Lowcountry and the country to find the best, locally sourced foods, produce, and seafood. The Johnson & Wales grad actually began his culinary career in Charleston, where he studied and later landed at **Anson** (see p. 40). He opened Sapphire Grill in 1998, where it has since been lauded by national press and Savannahians. The space is romantic and sophisticated, tucked behind **Lady & Sons** (p. 194) and enveloped in ancient brick walls that spire skyward in three long, narrow stories. Lighting is dim and the mood is sexy, further enhanced by Nason's stunning fare. The calamari is encrusted with benne seeds and drizzled with a toasted-coriander pesto and tossed with a zippy curried peanut, lime, sugar, and soy glaze. This dish really makes your mouth pop, while it's quieted with the soothing grilled ricotta cream bread tossed in a rustic salad with a lavender vinaigrette. New York strip, veal loin, lamb rack, black grouper, diver scallops, and tuna mignon are just some of what can be ordered from the prime meat and seafood dishes that are then paired with your choice of sauces (think truffle butter or wild-mushroom demi) and a choice of two sides, including the incredible melted tomato. Prices are higher here than most places around town, but you get what you pay for in flavor and ambience, rendering Sapphire Grill a definite spot on my Top Ten Must Do's List in Savannah.

Soho South Cafe, 12 W. Liberty St. (between Bull & Whitaker Streets), downtown Savannah, GA 31401; (912) 233-1633; www .sohosouthcafe.com; Soup/Sandwiches/Salads; $–$$. One part art studio, one part bohemian style, and one part super, super delicious food, Soho South wins in a big way, on all fronts. Add to that the fact that its situated right next door to an ultra-convenient parking lot, and overlooks a beautiful, shaded stretch of Liberty Street that looks like a slice out of Paris, and you've found a star Savannah breakfast or lunch destination. (Soho also does a hugely popular Sunday brunch with all kinds of egg and waffle and brioche French toast goodies). Settle under one of the skylights at an umbrella-covered bistro table and choose from an eclectic mix of homey favorites like moist and chunky meat loaf served on a fresh Kaiser roll and topped with Russian dressing, or go lighter and sample the out-of-this-world perfect grilled salmon BLT on a freshly baked challah roll topped with fresh-herbed mayo, bacon, arugula, and tomatoes. The ultimate comfort food resides in individual chicken potpies or a  four-cheese grilled cheese served with a steaming cup of Soho's justifiably celebrated tomato-basil bisque. There are several salads and quiches, options for those in search of lighter fare. Every option is a winner at Soho South Cafe and all are served by a congenial, informed staff, which is why Soho is on my Top Ten Must-Do's list for Savannah. Don't miss it!

STARLAND DISTRICT

This burgeoning little hot spot runs basically below 37th Street all the way to 45th Street between Habersham Street and Barnard Street. The neighborhood includes an eclectic group of eateries from the legendary **Elizabeth on 37th** (p. 193) to the divine little sweet spot, **Back in the Day Bakery** (p. 169). Scattered like so many green dice all the way in between are a number of socially and environmentally conscious restaurants, each serving their own brand of fresh deliciousness. If you're itching to get away from Southern and heavier fare and see another side of Savannah, Starland is the place to be. Because it's a few miles from historic downtown, getting there affords a driving or public transportation opportunity.

Sol Fusion Restaurant, 1611 Habersham St., downtown Savannah, GA 31401; (912) 232-1874; Tacos/Eclectic/Fusion; $$. Sol trots all over the globe, from Morocco to Jamaica, utilizing many techniques and ingredients in its whimsical, inventive menu. Sometimes there is just a little bit too much going on, but Fusion's fish tacos and especially the skirt-steak tacos really shine. The lime shimmers with acidic bite that surrounds the tender, marinated steak strips, getting a cooling hand from a cilantro-lime sour cream and avocado. A refreshing mint mojo sauce unites it with perfection. Sol has a utilitarian, former-filling-station look to it and an urban-chic feel that makes sense with its mostly younger clientele.

The Starland Cafe, 11 E. 41st St., Savannah (Starland District), GA 31401; (912) 443-9355; Soup/Sandwiches/Salads; $. Some of the most "thoughtfully hand-crafted menu items," as Starland Cafe's menu describes them, make their super-fresh and health-satisfying appearance at this rambling old blue Victorian house with a playful aqua trim. Orders are taken at a small counter that fronts the busy kitchen, and you serve your own sweet tea. Seating can be inside one of the many high-ceiling rooms or outside in the garden, laden with fresh herb pots and shading umbrellas, which also happens to overlook Savannah's Dog Park.

But pay attention when the food arrives—it's too good to miss even one of the many bright flavors. The stunning tomato Thai soup happens to be vegan, but tastes like a heavenly indulgence. The base is prepared with two different kinds of roasted squash pureed with toma-toes, seasoned with tongue-tingling Thai spices and rounded out with a dash of coconut cream. The kitchen-sink salad piles on the veggies with romaine, red grapes, asparagus, artichoke hearts, raisins, dates, red onion, green apple, and roasted tomatoes that crunch together merrily with Asian noodles and a smooth buttermilk dressing that gets a light infusion of tomato oil. It sounds like almost too much, but it's not. Starland is Savannah's shining star for garden-fresh goodness. Beefy, meaty panini options for meat lovers are sealed with fresh grilled ciabatta bread.

Wright Square Cafe, 21 W. York St., downtown Savannah, GA 31401; (912) 238-1150; Sandwiches/Chocolates; $. This calm and inviting little spot on the edge of pretty Wright Square has a soothing quality to it that makes you want to come in and stay a while. Wright Cafe does several things well, including smashing and inventive stuffed breakfast and lunch croissants (don't miss the curry chicken salad croissant with mango chutney!), pressed, cheesy panini on potato chive bread, and toothsome salads and quiches, but it's the chocolates here that steal the whole show. The face behind the chocolates is CIA (Hyde Park) grad and artisanal mastermind Adam Turoni. The talented chocolatier spins **Savannah Bee Company** honey (see p. 204) into chocolate in the shape of an adorable bee hive and bravely puts bacon and blue cheese in his dreamy truffles. Currently, Wright Square Cafe is his principal point of distribution. Purchase a pretty little box of his magnificent chocolates to take home, that is if you can resist eating them on the way.

Zunzi's, 108 E. York St., downtown Savannah, GA 31401; (912) 443-9555; www.zunzis.com; South African/Eclectic; $. It's a wrap and more at Zunzi's, a hot and happening South African sandwich shop where you can find everything from lasagna to curry stew. All are served with style and smiles from enthusiastic and friendly owners and husband-and-wife team Johnny and Gabriella DeBeer. Their international origins (his South Africa and hers Italy) collide deliciously at this mostly take-out corner, most easily identified by its many flags flying out front and the exotic scents—allspice, cloves, curry—emanating from the tiny kitchen all the way down East York Street. The house-made South African sausage served with gravy, sautéed onions, and mushrooms is especially noteworthy, as are Zunzi's zesty signature sauces that greedily drip from all the sandwiches and nearly everything served here, if you so choose. Hours can be a little unpredictable, so call ahead if you're thinking of stopping by during slower seasons (and here that means when school's out—SCAD students hang out here in throngs) or slower times of day for traditional eating. There is some seating on a patio outside if you decide to eat in.

Landmarks

Elizabeth on 37th, 105 E. 37th St., Savannah (Starland District), GA 31401; (912) 236-5547; www.elizabethon37th.net; Classic Southern Cuisine; $$$$. Elizabeth on 37th broke all kinds of Southern culinary ground when Elizabeth Terry and her husband opened their restaurant in 1981. The gorgeous old Georgian mansion (circa 1900) was then, as it is now, the perfect setting for her impeccably researched and executed 18th- and 19th-century Savannahian cooking. She brought it all to the plate with a style that embraced a deft lightness, a sweep of femininity, and a core of Southern culinary tradition, all with a modern edge. The world stood up and took notice, showering Chef Terry and her charming, bow-tie-clad staff with all kinds of awards, including the prestigious DiRoNA award for 14 years straight. Though Elizabeth has since retired her toque, her style of cooking and recipes continue in the able hands of Executive Chef Kelly Yambor. It's as if time has stopped here—quality and charm galore just keep on coming as they always have. The staff is adorable in their enthusiastic yet restrained approach. One server told me, as I bit into one of Elizabeth's celebrated and incredible cheese biscuits, "Excuse me while I interrupt your biscuit eating." I did, for his manners as much for the decadent biscuit that's even better slathered with fresh creamery butter and house-made marmalade. Fireplaces, high ceilings, dark walls, and ample antiques support the manner to which the old mansion is no doubt accustomed, and also add to a very special dining experience. Many of the vegetables and herbs come from the garden just behind the house and their freshness is remarkably apparent in every bite. The double-cut Berkshire pork chop served with a cheesy, gooey, five-cheese macaroni and amazing apple-cabbage slaw and the spicy Savannah red rice with Georgia shrimp are exceptional—but then, nothing disappoints here, only amazes. That's why Elizabeth on 37th is firmly planted among my Top Ten Must Do's in Savannah.

The Lady & Sons, 102 W. Congress St., downtown Savannah, GA 31401; (912) 233-2600; www.ladyandsons.com; Southern Comfort Food; $$. No offense to Paula Deen, y'all. I greatly respect the woman who raised her two sons on sandwiches she made and they sold—a business that eventually would morph into this successful restaurant, long a Savannah favorite. But then fame and travel and distractions inevitably arrived just as Paula's star reached its Food Network zenith. All power to her! But the restaurant, no matter what it was before, has become something of a Southern culinary theme park. A virtual army of staff and servers wear microphones and

earpieces as they herd the masses (and I mean masses) of people that line up on West Congress every morning to get a piece of Paula's pie. Seating begins at 11 a.m. and reservations (which you have to make that morning, ideally when the hostess arrives at 9:30 a.m.) are only taken for groups of six or more. Personally, I'd rather spend my time in a quieter, less commercialized setting (like at Mrs. Wilkes'), but, that said, once you get through all of that craziness, the food is solid enough to recommend it, especially to Paula Deen fans. The buffet is stacked with the usual suspects, some made in unusually delicious ways, such as the Southern fried chicken, which has deep, to-the-bone flavor and nice crunch, but with a much less made-to-order quality than Mrs. Wilkes'. Collards, mac and cheese, gooey butter cakes, and more are all in the buffet offing for roughly the same price as well, depending on what time of day or night you go. The a la carte menu is full of Paula classics like a deep-dish chicken potpie and "sho-nuff" vegetable sandwich.

Leopold's Ice Cream, 212 E. Broughton St., downtown Savannah, GA 31401; (912) 234-4442; www.leopoldsicecream.com; Ice Cream/Shakes/Sandwiches; $. This red-and-white candy-striped delight was originally founded in 1919 (at a different location) through the hard work and dedication of three Greek immigrant brothers. They honed the skills they learned from an uncle about making candies and desserts to create their unparalleled (indeed, some would call it legendary, myself included), house-made ice creams, malts, black-and-white sodas, and banana splits. Though the shop, in the heart of the retail district on Broughton, is now owned and operated by descendant and famed Hollywood producer Stratton Leopold and his wife, the creamy, cool, and delicious ice cream tradition continues. Line up at the counter to sample one of some 20 house-made varieties, place your order, and dig in. The iconic ice cream speaks of total dairy freshness, real ingredients, and zero chemical additives or emulsifiers. It is the real deal! The popular tutti frutti boasts colorful chunks of bubble gum while each bite of the celestial coconut ice cream melts into chewy little bites of the fresh stuff at the creamy finish. Leopold's also serves tempting Southern classic sandwiches like chicken salad and pimento cheese, but don't leave without dessert. The ice cream is out of this world and the recipes are top secret!

Mrs. Wilkes' Dining Room, 107 W. Jones St., downtown Savannah, GA 31401; (912) 232-5997; www.mrswilkes.com; Southern Comfort Food; $$. If a sweeter, more authentically Southern meal and all-around dining experience exists in the Lowcountry, I've yet to find it. Mrs. Wilkes' follows a unique plan in today's modern world, but its community-table essence is grounded in tradition. The dining room is situated in the basement of a large old brick boarding house on a leafy, quiet stretch of West Jones Street. The original Mrs. Wilkes, one Sema Wilkes, opened the boarding house and the dining room in 1943. In the latter, she served heaps of Southern classics to the boarders, platter style, and with maternal warmth. The tradition continues today, virtually untouched. The dining room serves from 11 a.m. to 2 p.m. sharp, Monday through Friday. There are no reservations and there is no preferential treatment. The line forms, usually about 10:30 a.m. and continues until after 2 p.m. when the last of those in line are finally fed. Normally I would say no to lines, having experienced too many of them in my life only to find tourist-trap food. Not so at Mrs. Wilkes'! During the wait, anticipation builds along with your appetite as the enticing scent of fried chicken and stewed butter beans perfume the air, and the patient masses engage in friendly small talk. When you reach the door (count on about an hour wait, give or take), you and the closest nine people around you are ushered to an open, large, dining table and seated. Sweet tea or water is served by a series of friendly servers and then the food starts coming. A grand total of twenty revolving platters and bowls of Southern staples, including quite possibly the world's best fried chicken, mashed potatoes, gravy, stewed tomatoes and okra, corn bread, meat loaf, barbecue and whatever else

you're lucky to get that day, suddenly appear. The meal and the breaking of the bread become a kind of family affair, except minus the drama that sometimes exists with real family with the congeniality that comes with the new friends (and surrogate family) you are sure to make here. Afterward, you're kindly asked to clear your plate when you're finished and you pay a very gentle $16 in cash (no credit cards) as you leave, invariably with a huge smile upon your face, one very happy belly, and very nap ready. This is why Mrs. Wilkes' Dining Room takes a high place on my Top Ten Must Do's Savannah list. Note, the menu changes daily, but, happily fried chicken is always on the list.

The Olde Pink House, 23 Abercorn St., downtown Savannah, GA 31401; (912) 232-4286; Southern/Seafood; $$–$$$. The old girl's been here a long time, since 1771 in fact. Her bright pink paint and prominent position facing Reynolds Square make her hard to miss. Her colonial past is still very much alive in the look and feel of the place, with long, fat, heart-pine planks and several antique fireplaces. The restaurant meanders from dining room to dining room in true period fashion, each with a slightly modified color scheme, but all with chandeliers, long drapes, and wooden captain's chairs. Downstairs is the more relaxed Planter's Tavern with huge arched windows that look out onto Julian Street. It feels part bar and part business lunch spot, filling up with lots of suits and bow ties come midday. The mood is very masculine with the heavy weight of imposing, medieval-looking chandeliers and hunting-themed art, and the place smells a little sweet and sticky, as bars sometimes do.

But, the food comes from the same kitchen as the dining room, and it's good stuff, starting with the exceptional, crisp cheese straws served in a pewter cup. The lunch menu (dinner is also served) is eclectic, with lots of Southern staples (crab cakes, shrimp and grits, shrimp gumbo, country fried chicken, fried seafood platter), but also has several more modern touches in the yummy Asian beef salad and fish tacos. The fried chicken chop salad is a delicious blend of fresh veggies, blue cheese, bacon, and chunks of fried chicken tossed in one of the best dressings I've ever had, the house red-wine vinaigrette—which is, of course, pink,

mild, and slightly acidic, not unlike The Olde Pink House herself. A true Savannah classic, make reservations here for both lunch and dinner. She fills up fast day and night.

700 Drayton Restaurant, Mansion on Forsyth Park, 700 Drayton St., downtown Savannah, GA 31401; (912) 721-5002; www.mansion onforsythpark.com; Southern/Eclectic; $$$–$$$$. Originally a family residence when it was built in 1888, this architectural tour de force eventually became a mortuary, then a synagogue, then it was vacant until it was revived as a Kessler hotel and a restaurant. Talk about skeletons in the closet! If there are any resident ghosts, the colorful, Mardi Gras–like art and dark velvet draperies no doubt keep them at bay. The more formal dining room has a staid but pleasant aura, while the upstairs bar and alfresco lounge afford sweeping vistas of lovely Forsyth Park. The menu is eclectic, and for the most part can be ordered no matter what dining nook you choose, since food from any of the menus can be served no matter where you're seated. The pan-seared bass with a cilantro truffle oil, balsamic reduction, mashed potatoes, and asparagus was smashing, but I also enjoyed the calamari, which was full of huge Mediterranean flavor, mostly in a tapenade-like topping prepared with olive, asiago, coriander, fresh cilantro, and a saffron-threaded aioli. Delicious! Specialty drinks and cool, sophisticated service add a special touch to the 700 Drayton experience.

The Tea Room, 7 E. Broughton St., downtown Savannah, GA 31401; (912) 239-9690; www.thetearoomsavannah.com; Tea/Sandwiches; $–$$$. This gem of a tea shop, led by one Elizabeth Ruby, is a true Savannahian destination for a well-steeped pot of assorted teas and all kinds of goodies on a three-tiered tray. High tea, served after 2:30 p.m. and with a reservation, is an event not soon forgotten. The cool refuge of the library room makes for a quiet and soothing respite any time of year. The larger dining area is encompassed by a shopping area filled with tea cozies, frilly aprons, and whatever your heart desires, really. If tea, specifically, is not your fancy, opt for the delightful lunch menu, which affords a tasty egg salad sandwich (oh, so Southern) or plump, grilled shrimp Caesar salad. The Tea Room is, for all the reasons stated above, and many more, a primary destination. Mark it, as I do, as one of Savannah's Top 10 Must Do's. The Tea Room has personality plus and more to spare!

Vic's On the River, 26 E. Bay St. and 15 E. River St., downtown Savannah, GA 31401; (912) 721-1000; www.VicsOnTheRiver.com; Southern/Seafood/Steak; $$$. This 5-story building, built in 1859, just before the start of the Civil War, is structurally something of an enigma. It scales the Savannah River north bank a total of 4 stories. At the rear, the entrance is on the true ground level at River Street, which requires taking an elevator to the main dining room, or you can enter at what seems like ground level (but it's actually the 4th floor!) at the front entrance on East Bay Street. Vic's prime riverfront locale attracts hordes of tourists and the unfortunate requisite tacky tourist attractions, but Vic's truly stands apart as a first-class dining destination for tourists and locals alike. Inside feels like a cool, soothing oasis with crisp, cosmopolitan hues of black and white, live nightly piano music, and huge, arched windows framing beautiful bird's-eye views of the river. The menu affords many choices across many price ranges, even conveniently adding a simple menu of evening sandwiches and a plate of four side dishes (don't miss the smoked-cheddar grits) for diners to mix and match when appetites are not quite up to rib eye or high-price-point snuff. Begin with a cocktail at the sexy, well-stocked bar to shake off the stress of the day. The cakey, sweet biscuits that begin each meal are addictive. Vic's version of fried green tomatoes is delicate and delicious. Three little lightly battered and fried discs are neatly stacked on a small pool of grits and topped with a dollop of goat cheese and sweet/tart tomato chutney. Also on the appetizer menu are delightfully interpreted pulled-pork fried egg rolls stuffed with oh-so-tender pork with three zippy dipping options: barbecue sauce, hot mustard, and lovely peach chutney. Entrees call on big, hungry-man appetite guns with the likes of the scored, glazed, crunchy flounder and Southern-fried pork chops with a sweet onion gravy.

Specialty Stores, Markets & Producers

Charles J. Russo Seafood, 201 E. 40th St. (at Abercorn), downtown Savannah, GA 31401; (912) 234-5196 or toll free (866) 234-5196; www.russoseafood.com. Wholesale/Retail seafood. For over 60 years, Russo's has delivered the freshest local fish to restaurants and home kitchens alike. A bit tattered and torn from the outside, complete with a "shadow" fishing boat with life-size fishermen, inside it gleams with fresh shrimp, whole flounder, spottail bass, and whatever the bounty of the sea issued into fishermen's nets earlier that day. Fresh ice is constantly being added to the fish beds to ensure freshness. Bypass the unremarkable Russo's restaurant next door and shop here for some fresh fish, take it home, and cook it up. (Or opt for one of the prepared dishes, such as the legendary deviled crabs from owner Charles Russo Jr.'s own mother's recipe box.) Dress it with some of Russo's tangy and delicious tartar sauce for an authentically Savannahian feast.

The Distillery, 416 W. Liberty St., downtown Savannah, GA 31401; (912) 236-1772; www.distillerysavannah.com; Craft Beer. The second time is the charm for this fabulous craft beer destination located in an old building (circa 1904) that was originally a bourbon distillery. Craft beer enthusiasts Michael and Lori Valen create ales, stouts, and beer in house and present a rotating total of 21 different choices to their ardent fans on any given day. With names like Stone Pale Ale and Lost Abbey Judgment Day, the brew goes down smoothly with tasty pub food that is also available at The Distillery.

Ogeechee River Coffee Company, 4517 Habersham St., Savannah (Habersham Village), GA 31405; (912) 354-7420; www.ogeecheecoffee.com; Fresh Roasted Artisanal Coffee/Cafe. The scent of roasted coffee that wafts through this sprightly little cafe in Habersham Village (a few miles south of downtown) makes java junkies weak in the knees. The beans are hand-selected and imported from exotic locations like Bali, Costa Rica, and Panama and roasted daily at a nearby roasting house. The results are astounding— smoky, deep flavors from every different bean. Favorites on the specialty drink list include the Sun & Moon, which merges white and dark chocolate to make mocha, and the Big Kahuna, a sultry blend of macadamia, white chocolate, and coffee. A small selection of sandwiches and salads is also offered, but it's really all about the coffee at Ogeechee.

River Street Sweets, 13 E. River St., downtown Savannah, GA 31401; (912) 234-4608; www.riverstreetsweets.com; Candy/ Chocolates. What began as a small family
business on River Street in 1973 has
morphed into a candy empire, with
locations all over the Southeast
(including Charleston at the corner
of Market and King Streets). The
original Savannah location is worth a
look-see, just to experience the whole
Willy Wonka-ness of it all. Follow
the candy making trail throughout
the winding store and don't leave
until you've had one of River Street's
world-famous (for a reason!), simply
gorgeous pralines.

Savannah Bee Company, 104 W. Broughton St., downtown Savannah, GA 31401; (800) 955-5080; www.savannahbee.com; Artisanal Honey Foods & Soaps. The buzz is on and the word is honey at Savannah Bee Company. Owner and beekeeper Ted Dennard loves his bees and his honey. A wedge of honeycomb and a menu of cool drinks greet visitors at the door in this sunny shop which all but glows with the amber hues of honey, beautifully bottled and displayed on the walls. There is honey for all occasions—grilling, tea, cheese, and the celebrated Tupelo, orange blossom, and black sage varieties. It is magnificent honey! There are also beauty and health products made from the honey and kids will love the larger-than-life-size walk-in beehive where education videos about beekeeping and honey-making play all day. There are two other locations in Savannah, but this is the most compelling. There is also a new Savannah Bee Company store in Charleston. It's located at 216 King St., downtown Charleston, 29401.

Two Smart Cookies, 6512 White Bluff Rd. (1 block north of Stephenson Ave.), Savannah, GA 31405; (912) 353-BAKE; www .twosmartcookies.com; Specialty Cookies. Another venture that started small and got big because their cut-out cookies are so darn beautiful and delicious, Two Smart Cookies still has a shop on White Bluff Road a little outside of downtown. Their flaky, cut-out butter cookies show off all kinds of pretty shapes—hearts, flowers, stars, circles, and more—that are painted in beautiful shades of pastel frosting and other dainty, flirty styles. I first encountered them by chance at the Paris Market at 36 W. Broughton St., downtown Savannah, GA 31401. There is a fabulous little cafe in the corner of this French-themed boutique store that is well worth a visit to sate the Francophile in everyone. And you can get the cookies there, too.

Road Trip! Beautiful Beaufort, SC

Located about halfway between Charleston and Savannah, Beaufort (pronounced "bwew-fert") is a beautiful, small historic town surrounded by water. It's a perfect destination for a day trip from either city or a stopping point while driving through from either one. Beaufort can be accessed from I-95 (via 278) or from Highway 17 (via Route 21). Either route is lovely, but the marsh and Lowcountry scenery off of 278 is breathtaking. I would argue that it's one of the most beautiful drives in this beautiful country and definitely in the Lowcountry. Beaufort is very old and historic, chartered in 1711. It's a lovely city for walking and exploring by foot. The old city actually sits on an island (Port Royal Island) and is also surrounded by islands, including nearby Sea Island. That's where you'll find Gullah Grub, a delightful and authentic spot for lunching on Lowcountry classics like fried shrimp and chunky **Fish Chowder** (the recipe is on p. 230). **Gullah Grub Restaurant,** 877 Sea Island Pkwy., St. Helena Island, SC, 29920; (843) 838-3841; Southern/Seafood; $–$$.

Learn to Cook

Foody Tours, (888) 653-6045; www.savannahtours.com. This ultra-fun tour for diehard foodies takes a small group through historic Savannah to tour and taste from 7 select restaurants and specialty shops from a total list of 21 that they visit on a rotation and availability basis. Taste and tour away for 2½ to 3 hours while taking in Savannah's scenery. Reservations must be made in advance.

The 700 Kitchen Cooking School, 700 Drayton St. (The Mansion on Forsyth Park), downtown Savannah, GA 34101; (912) 721-5043; www.mansionforsythpark.com. Enjoy hands-on, intimate cooking classes at this state-of-the-art kitchen located within the mansion itself. Culinary Director–Chef Darin Sehnert spearheads a wonderful program of delightful classes like Summer Picnic, Father's Day Feast, and Lowcountry Cooking that rotate with the season. Individual or group classes are available. Classes need to be reserved in advance. It's not required that you be a guest at The Mansion to participate!

Recipes

Charleston and Savannah prove they are not home to just barbecue and fried chicken, though both can be found in good measure in both cities. The diversity of both cities, in embracing new and old ideas, new and old ingredients, and most frequently these days, locally sourced products, truly resonates in the assortment of recipes to follow in this chapter. Whether a simple sampler of spiced Georgia nuts or a decadent red velvet pound cake, delicious goodness reigns, just like Charleston and Savannah themselves.

Bull Street Gourmet's
Famous Chicken Salad

The sweetness of dried cranberries helps the mellow flavor of the slow-roasted chicken pop in this Bull Street Gourmet classic. At the shop, it can be ordered by quart-size container or on a fresh baguette. It also makes a great topper for a bed of lightly dressed greens.

Makes 8 servings

1 4 to 4½ pound whole chicken
Salt and freshly ground pepper
1 cup whole almonds
2 cups best quality mayonnaise
(suggest Duke's)

1 cup Craisins brand dried
cranberries
Salt and freshly ground pepper
to taste

Preheat oven to 375 degrees. Meanwhile lightly rinse the chicken under the tap and then pat thoroughly dry using paper towels. Season the chicken liberally with salt and pepper in the chest cavity and all over the body of the chicken. Roast in a roasting pan on the lower rack of the oven until the juices run clear when the chicken is pierced with a knife, about 1 hour and 15 minutes. (Note: You're shooting for an internal temperature of 165 degrees). Remove the chicken from the oven and allow to rest until cool enough to handle. While it's resting, heat a medium skillet over medium-high heat. Add 1 cup whole almonds to the pan and toast, tossing occasionally, until they start turning

a light golden color and give off a sweet, almond aroma. Remove from heat and set aside.

When the chicken's cool, remove all of the skin from the chicken and discard, along with any excess fat or sinew. Pick the flesh off all of the bones and place in a large bowl, discarding the bones. Using a fork, "pull" the chicken into long strands. Turn out on a cutting board and chop coarsely, if desired. To finish the salad, combine the prepared chicken with the mayonnaise in a large bowl, stirring thoroughly to combine. Coarsely chop the almonds and fold into the mixture along with the Craisins and salt and freshly ground pepper to taste.

At Bull Street Gourmet, they serve the salad as is on a few leaves of lettuce or place it between some delicious, fresh white bread for sandwiches. It can be stored safely in the refrigerator in an airtight container for up to 3 days.

Courtesy of Justin Croxall/Bull Street Gourmet, Charleston (p. 24).

Caviar & Bananas'
Broccoli & Lentil Salad

Caviar & Bananas' Executive Chef Todd Mazurek was kind enough to share his fabulous recipe for his chewy, lemony, rich lentil salad. Meyer lemons are sweeter and less acidic than regular lemons. They're in season in cooler months, from November to May. If you can't find them, substitute 1 teaspoon of the lemon juice with fresh squeezed orange juice. Beluga lentils are dark and chewy and so named because they resemble the caviar by the same name. Substitute French green lentils if you can't track down the beluga variety.

Serves 8 to 10

2 cups uncooked beluga lentils

1 cup cooked, diced bacon

2 cups raw broccoli, rinsed and thinly sliced, or broken into small florets (discard tough stems)

1½ cups ripe Roma tomatoes (or another vine-ripe tomato), diced

1 cup blue cheese, crumbled

½ cup toasted pine nuts

3 tablespoons best quality (first press if possible) extra virgin olive oil

2 teaspoons fresh squeezed Meyer lemon juice (about half of a Meyer lemon)

Salt and freshly ground pepper to taste

Bring a large pot of cold water to a boil over high heat. Add the lentils and cook at a boil for 10 to 12 minutes or until they're tender and cooked through. Drain the lentils using a colander and rinse thoroughly with cold water to stop

the cooking process. Set aside. While the lentils are cooking, prep the additional salad ingredients. When the lentils are well drained and cooled to room temperature, combine them in a large bowl with the prepped bacon, broccoli, tomatoes, blue cheese, and pine nuts, tossing gently with a wooden spoon. Add the olive oil and lemon juice; toss to coat. Season generously with salt and freshly ground pepper. Taste carefully and adjust seasonings as needed. Serve slightly cool or at room temperature. The salad will keep up to 24 hours in the refrigerator in an airtight container. Delicious with a fresh baguette for a satisfying meal!

Courtesy of Todd Mazurek/Caviar & Bananas Gourmet Market & Cafe, Charleston (p. 26).

Dixie Cafe Shrimp "BLFGT" Sandwich

The Holmeses say to "go out and get the freshest local shrimp you can find" for their show-stopping Shrimp, Bacon, Lettuce & Fried Green Tomato Sandwich.

Makes 6 BIG sandwiches

For the tomatoes:

3 large green tomatoes cut into 4 thick slices each (for a total of 12 slices)

1 cup buttermilk

2 cups all-purpose flour

1 cup yellow cornmeal (local stone ground is best!)

1 teaspoon onion powder

1 teaspoon garlic powder

1 teaspoon paprika

Salt and freshly ground black pepper to taste

1½ cups canola or vegetable oil

For the shrimp:

24 strips bacon

1½ pounds large, fresh shrimp, peeled and deveined

Salt and freshly ground black pepper

To assemble the sandwiches:

12 slices fresh wheat-berry or whole-grain bread

6 tablespoons mayonnaise

6 to 12 leaves fresh Bibb or romaine lettuce

Reserved bacon, shrimp, and green tomatoes

Slice and set aside the tomatoes. Pour the buttermilk into a shallow bowl or soup plate. Combine the flour, cornmeal, onion powder, garlic powder, paprika, and salt and pepper on a plate or in a shallow bowl, whisking to blend. Dip each tomato slice in the buttermilk and then dredge it in the flour/seasoning mixture, tapping off excess. Heat the oil in a deep skillet over medium-high heat (or to 325 degrees if using a deep fryer) until bubbling. Place the tomatoes in the hot oil in a single layer without crowding. Fry until golden and crisp, turning once. This should take about 5 minutes.

Meanwhile, heat a large, deep frying pan over medium-high heat. Arrange the bacon in a single layer and cook until golden and crisp, turning once, about 5 minutes total. Drain the bacon on paper towels once cooked. Reserve 4 table-spoons of the bacon fat. In a second large sauté pan, heat the reserved bacon fat over medium-high heat. Season the shrimp liberally with salt and pepper. Place them in the hot pan and sauté until golden on the outside and just opaque in the center—about 3 minutes. Do not overcook! Remove from the pan and drain on paper towels.

To compile the sandwiches, arrange 6 slices of the bread on your work surface. Slather liberally with the mayonnaise. Top each with a leaf or two of lettuce, 4 strips of crisp bacon, 2 slices of crisp, fried green tomatoes, 4 or 5 sautéed shrimp, and the remaining slice of bread.

At Dixie Cafe, the sandwiches are sliced diagonally and served with homemade pickles.

Courtesy of Kris and Allen Holmes/Dixie Supply Bakery & Cafe, Charleston (p. 27).

Hominy Grill's Cheese Grits

These cheesy, toothsome grits are like an indulgent, savory pudding. Top them with whatever you like, or serve them as is, with a side of scrambled eggs and bacon. For more on grits, see Puttin' on the Grits (p. 41). From the restaurant's cookbook, Recipes from Hominy Grill: *"When I was a child, we always bought our grits from the Old Mill of Guilford in Oak Ridge, NC. We still get them there today. They are stone ground from fling corn and have a warm flavor of the summer sun."*

Serves 6

4½ cups water
1 cup stone-ground grits
1 teaspoon salt
¾ cup grated sharp cheddar
   cheese

¼ cup grated **Parmesan** cheese
3 tablespoons butter
½ teaspoon freshly ground
   pepper
½ teaspoon Tabasco

In a medium saucepan over high heat, bring water to a boil. Whisk in the grits and the salt, reduce heat to low, and cook, stirring occasionally, until the grits are thickened, approximately 35 to 40 minutes. Remove from the heat and add the cheeses, butter, pepper, and Tabasco, adding more to adjust seasoning as desired.

Courtesy of Robert Stehling Hominy Grill, Charleston (p. 80).

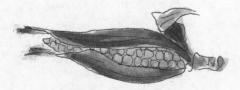

Hot Pickled Okra Bloody Marys

Ryan Roberts and Ryan Eleuteri of Charleston Bloody Mary Mix generously created this original recipe expressly for this book. They make their own pickled okra and spice up vodka with a jalapeño infusion. You can take a few shortcuts and buy your own pickled okra (or substitute pickled green beans) and buy vodka that's already spiked with heat. It's extra fun to make your own, though, if you think of it ahead of time. As far as the suggested vodka brand to use, Eleuteri recommends both Svedka and Ketel One for their "clean tastes."

Makes 6 generous Bloody Marys

For the Okra Pickles:

Equipment needed: 3 1-pint, sterile Mason jars

1½ pounds fresh okra, rinsed and trimmed

3 dried red chile peppers

3 teaspoons dried dill

2 cups water

1 cup vinegar

2 teaspoons salt

For the Jalapeño Vodka:

2 jalapeños, thinly sliced

1 bottle (750 ml) vodka (Note: You will have some leftover.)

For the Bloody Marys:

4 cups Charleston Bloody Mary Mix

1⅓ cups jalapeño vodka

½ cup fresh lemon juice

½ cup okra pickling liquid

At least 3 to 4 days in advance, prepare the okra pickles and jalapeño vodka. For the pickles, divide the okra evenly among 3 sterile, 1-pint jars. Pack loosely into the jars and add 1 dried chile and 1 teaspoon of dried dill to each jar. Meanwhile, in a small saucepan, combine the water, vinegar, and salt. Bring to a boil over high heat. Divide the mixture among the prepared jars, cover with lids, and seal in a hot water bath for 10 minutes. Reserve at room temperature or refrigerated until ready to use. Remember to refrigerate any open jars after opening. To prepare the jalapeño vodka, simply add the sliced jalapeños to the vodka in its bottle, return the cap, and store in a dark place for 3 to 4 days.

To make the Bloody Marys, simply combine the Charleston Bloody Mary Mix, jalapeño vodka, lemon juice, and juice from okra pickles (or substitute store bought pickled veggies) in a large pitcher and chill. Serve over ice if desired and garnish with one or two pickled okra.

Courtesy of Ryan Roberts and Ryan Eleuteri/Charleston Bloody Mary Mix (p. 84).

Sarah's Red Velvet Pound Cake

Generously shared by Sarah O'Kelley: "Mystery surrounds the Red Velvet Cake; the particulars of its origin and ingredients vary from cook to cook. But any bona-fide Southerner better have one in their repertoire. Mine comes in the form of a pound cake, as I feel the density stands up beautifully to all that cream cheese frosting! And I certainly don't go light on the food coloring, since red is the point, after all.

Makes 8 servings

For the cake:

Softened butter for pan

2½ cups sugar

8 large eggs

1 14-ounce can condensed milk

1 tablespoon vanilla extract

2 teaspoons kosher salt

1 pound unsalted butter, melted

2¼ cups cake flour

¾ cup unsweetened cocoa powder, plus more for pan

2 teaspoons baking powder

½ cup red food coloring

Preheat oven to 350 degrees. Grease a standard-size Bundt pan with softened butter and then dust with cocoa powder.

Combine sugar, eggs, condensed milk, vanilla, and salt in a food processor; mix until combined. While the processor is running, pour in melted butter and continue running until thoroughly combined. Pour this mixture into a large mixing bowl. Sift flour, cocoa powder, and baking powder into the mixture, whisking as you go. Add red food coloring; whisk to combine. Pour batter into prepared pan.

Bake until a toothpick inserted into the center comes out clean, about 1½ hours. Remove from the oven and cool for 10 minutes. Release the cake from the pan onto a serving plate. Allow to thoroughly cool. Applying frosting to a cake is a battle against crumbs. It is easier done when the cake is cold, so refrigerate the cake until well chilled. Meanwhile, prepare the frosting.

Cream Cheese Frosting

24 ounces cream cheese, softened

15 tablespoons unsalted butter, softened

2¼ cups powdered sugar, sifted

2 tablespoons vanilla extract

2 tablespoons fresh lemon juice

Combine the cream cheese and butter in a large bowl and beat with an electric mixer until smooth and fluffy, 2 to 3 minutes. Add the sugar, vanilla, and lemon juice and mix on low speed until combined. Note: The icing can be made in advance and refrigerated, but should be brought to room temperature before using.

To frost the cake: *Remove the chilled cake from the refrigerator and apply a thin layer of Cream Cheese Frosting using an icing spatula. Return the cake to the refrigerator until the frosting hardens. Remove cake and apply remaining frosting using an icing spatula. Refrigerate until frosting stiffens up a bit. Slice while cold, but cake is best served at room temperature.*

Courtesy of Sarah O'Kelley/The Glass Onion, West Ashley, SC (p. 141).

Pan-Roasted Diver Scallops with Bacon & Corn Risotto

At Noble Fare, Chef McNamara serves this dish with a corn relish, balsamic reduction, basil oil, and a citrus-lime butter. However, in the interest of simplifying work for the home cook, we're simply including the recipe for the scallops and the corn risotto. You'll need to go to the restaurant to experience it exactly the way McNamara prepares it. Find the freshest scallops and corn you can find. McNamara makes his own chicken stock. Feel free to make your own or buy the best quality, sodium-free version available. This is simply delicious and very much a summer kind of dish.

Serves 4

For the bacon and corn risotto:

- 2 ears of corn, in husk
- 2 strips applewood smoked bacon
- 1 tablespoon butter
- ¼ cup diced Vidalia or sweet white onion
- ½ cup carnaroli (or substitute arborio) rice
- Kosher and freshly ground white pepper to taste
- ¼ cup dry white wine
- 2 cups warm chicken stock
- 1 to 2 tablespoons grated gruyère cheese

For the scallops:

- 16 fresh scallops
- Kosher salt and ground white pepper to season
- 4 tablespoon canola oil
- ½ cup clarified butter

Begin with the risotto. Preheat oven to 350 degrees and place the corn, husks on, on a baking sheet and bake for 25 minutes. Cool for 25 minutes, or until cool enough to handle. Remove the silk and husk, and cut the corn from the cob. Reserve the corn in a medium bowl and set aside. Meanwhile, cook the bacon over medium-high heat until crisp. Drain the bacon on paper towels and dice very fine. Set aside next to the corn. To prepare the risotto, heat the butter in a medium, deep-sided saucepan over medium heat. Add the butter and the diced onion. Cook, stirring, until the onion starts to soften, about 5 minutes. Add the rice, salt, and pepper, stir and cook until the rice starts to give off a toasted fragrance, about 3 to 5 minutes. Add the wine, stirring, and cook until all or most of the wine has been absorbed. Add the hot chicken stock in ½-cup increments, stirring as you go, until the stock is fully absorbed. Continue adding the stock until it's gone and the rice is creamy in texture and has absorbed the stock, about 20 to 25 minutes. Taste and adjust seasoning with salt and pepper as needed. Stir in the gruyère and reserved cooked corn and bacon. Cover and keep warm while preparing the scallops.

To prepare the scallops, pat them dry with a paper towel and season on both sides with salt and pepper. Heat a cast-iron skillet (or another type of large, heavy skillet, if you have to substitute) over high heat for 5 minutes. Cook the scallops in batches, four at a time. Put four scallops into the pan along with 1 tablespoon canola oil and 2 tablespoons clarified butter. Cook on one side for 2 minutes. Don't touch the scallops, turn off heat, and let rest in the pan for 1 minute. Remove to a plate and keep warm by lightly covering with aluminum foil as you cook the remaining scallops.

To serve, arrange a bed of the risotto on a plate and arrange four scallops around it. Garnish with fresh herbs if desired.

Courtesy of Patrick McNamara/Noble Fare, Savannah (p. 184).

Lulu's Savannah Bourbon Bellini

This smooth, smooth bellini brings together the Southern sweetness of bourbon and peaches and adds the refreshing touch of bubbles for the coolest, most refreshing drink for a hot summer night.

Serves 6

¾ **cup Woodford Reserve Bourbon**

¾ **cup Stirrings Peach Liqueur**

2¼ **cups Spanish cava or another good quality, dry sparkling wine**

6 **slices from one fresh peach for garnish**

Combine all in a large, tall pitcher. Serve over ice in 6 large white-wine glasses and garnish each with a fresh peach slice.

Courtesy of Lulu's Chocolate Bar, Savannah (p. 183).

Spiced Georgia Nuts

Green Truck Pub owner Joshua Yates says that "timing" is the secret to this recipe. "The nuts must be hot out of the oven when you mix them with the melted butter mixture or else it won't adhere, and you end up with dry nuts and clumps of spiced sugar."

Serves 6 to 8

- 1½ cups local pecan halves
- 1½ cups walnut halves
- 3½ tablespoons unsalted butter
- 2½ tablespoons light brown sugar
- 1 teaspoon cayenne pepper
- 2 tablespoons fresh rosemary, finely minced
- 1½ teaspoons coarse sea salt or kosher salt (or salt to taste)

Preheat the oven to 375 degrees. Arrange the nuts on a sheet pan and toast/roast until the nuts are warm and fragrant, 4 to 5 minutes. Meanwhile melt the butter and brown sugar together in a small saucepan. Remove the nuts from the oven and combine in a large mixing bowl with the melted butter and sugar, tossing thoroughly to coat. Return nuts to the baking sheet and toast/roast for another 3 to 5 minutes. Remove from the oven and return the nuts to the bowl. Toss with the remaining ingredients. Spread them out on the sheet pan and allow to cool completely so they do not clump together. Store in sealed container at room temperature for up to 2 days. These make excellent nibbles to go with cocktails or a great crunch to top a salad.

Courtesy of Joshua Yates/Green Truck Pub, Savannah (p. 178).

Cafe 37's Duck Liver Mousse
with Cherry Gastrique

This is much easier to make than the name implies. Serve the mousse on toasted French baguette croutons. Ras el Hanout is a North African spice blend that can be found from various Internet searches or specialty spice shops. Chef Elsinghorst prefers the way it lifts the flavor of the liver, but if you can't find it, substitute Four Spice Powder.

Serves 6

For the mousse:

½ pound (2 sticks) unsalted butter

1 pound duck livers (or substitute chicken livers), removing any dark or fatty spots

1 large egg

2 teaspoons salt

2 teaspoons Ras el Hanout

Bourbon (Bulleit brand if possible)

For the gastrique:

1 cup raspberry vinegar

½ cup granulated sugar

½ cup dried cherries

Preheat oven to 325 degrees. Melt the butter in a small saucepan over low heat. In a blender or food processor, combine the livers, egg, salt, Ras el Hanout, and bourbon. Pulse/blend until very fine and well combined. Once the butter has melted, slowly stream it into the blender/processor and blend on high until fully incorporated. Spray 6½-cup ramekins with a nonstick spray. Pour the mousse into each, filling each just halfway. Arrange the ramekins in a baking pan and fill the pan to half the height of the ramekins with warm water. Place the pan in the oven and bake for 20 to 25 minutes or until the centers have puffed slightly. Remove ramekins from the baking pan, arrange on a tray, and refrigerate for at least 30 minutes.

Meanwhile, prepare the gastrique. Combine the vinegar and sugar in a small saucepan. Cook over medium heat until reduced by half. Add the cherries. Keep warm until ready to serve. To serve, unmold each mousse from the ramekin by running a paring knife around the edges of the mold. Turn out onto a plate and top with warm (not super hot!) gastrique and freshly ground black pepper.

Courtesy of Blake Elsinghorst/Cafe 37, Savannah (p. 173).

Jazz'd Chicken Lettuce Wrap
with Peanut Curry Sauce

Thoroughly addictive and fairly easy to make, you'll find yourself wanting to return to these (or Jazz'd) again and again for a wrap fix.

Serves 6 to 8

10 cloves garlic, finely chopped

2 tablespoons crushed red pepper flakes

1½ cups teriyaki sauce

½ cup extra virgin olive oil

2½ pounds boneless, skinless chicken breasts

3 tablespoons extra virgin olive oil

2 leeks, well washed and sliced thinly into rings

2 red bell peppers, cored, halved, seeded, and cut into thin strips

½ cup dry roasted, unsalted peanuts

3 jalapeño peppers, cored, halved, seeded, and cut into thin strips

½ cup teriyaki sauce

For the lettuce wraps and garnish:

2 heads romaine lettuce leaves, well washed and dried

¼ cup shredded red cabbage

3 carrots, peeled and shredded

2 red onions, peeled and thinly sliced

For the sauce:

1 14-ounce can coconut milk

2 tablespoons red curry paste

2 tablespoons creamy peanut butter

Pinch cayenne pepper

¼ cup water

3 tablespoons cornstarch

The day before cooking/serving, combine the garlic, crushed red pepper flakes, 1½ cups teriyaki sauce and ½ cup extra virgin olive oil in a large mixing bowl. Add the chicken breasts and toss gently. Cover with plastic wrap and refrigerate overnight to marinate.

The following day, remove the chicken from the marinade, pat dry, and grill or sauté over medium-high heat for 4 to 5 minutes on each side until cooked through. Slice into thin strips and reserve. Separately, heat the 3 tablespoons extra virgin olive oil in a large sauté pan over medium heat. Add the leeks, red peppers, peanuts, and jalapeños and cook together for 2 minutes, tossing regularly. Add the reserved chicken breast strips and the ½ cup teriyaki sauce and cook until the sauce is completely absorbed. Serve the wraps with a heaping filling of the warm chicken mixture topped with the fresh, shredded veggies and a side of the sauce.

To make the sauce:

Combine all of the ingredients except the cornstarch and water in a medium saucepan and bring to a boil over high heat. Separately, combine the water and cornstarch in a small bowl, whisking to combine. Pour the mixture into the boiling coconut-milk sauce and whisk until thickened, 2 minutes. Serve warm.

Courtesy of Brian Gonet/Jazz'd Tapas Bar, Savannah (p. 181).

Gullah Grub's Fish Chowder

Gullah Grub owner Bubba Green says this is a labor-intensive recipe. Basically, it requires a lot of stirring throughout the whole process. He recommends using a 2-gallon pot, a large slotted spoon, and a large flat spoon. The results are worth the work!

Serves 6 to 8

1½ quarts canned, plain tomato puree

3 cups water

1 cup chopped onion

1 cup chopped celery

2 teaspoons chopped garlic

Juice of 1 lemon

2 teaspoons kosher salt

2 teaspoons ground black pepper

1½ teaspoons dried thyme

1½ teaspoons ground ginger

2 pounds coarsely chopped catfish filets (preferably wild and fresh)

Bring tomato puree and water to a low boil in a large stockpot over medium-high heat. Add the onion, celery, garlic, and lemon juice. Stir well until combined. Add the remaining ingredients (except the fish) and cook, stirring, for 10 minutes. Add the fish and cook an additional 6 to 10 minutes. Use the slotted and flat spoons to break apart the fish until all the chunks are broken down to very small pieces. Simmer for an additional 10 minutes. Serve very hot.

Courtesy of Bubba Green/Gullah Grub, St. Helena Island, SC (p. 206).

Appendices

Appendix A: Eateries by Cuisine

American

Charleston

Blu Restaurant & Bar, 122

Dining Room at The Woodlands/
    The Pines, The, 96

Marina Variety Store Restaurant, 34

Palmetto Cafe, 35

Rita's Seaside Grille, 126

Bakery

Charleston

Bakehouse, 21

Cupcake, 66

Dixie Supply Bakery & Cafe, 27

Macaroon Boutique, 69

Sugar Bakeshop, 76

WildFlour Pastry, 78

Savannah

Back in the Day Bakery, 169

Harris Baking Company, 180

Papillote, 185

Barbecue

Charleston

Fiery Ron's Home Team
    BBQ, 136

Pink Pig Bar & Q by Jim 'N
    Nick's, 38

Po' Pigs Bo-B-Q, 144

Savannah

Angel's BBQ, 169

Blowin' Smoke BBQ, 171

Beer Bar

Charleston
Closed for Business, 65
Gene's Haufbrau, 141
Smoky Oak Taproom, 127

Burgers

Charleston
Matt's Burgers, 93
Moe's Crosstown Tavern, 70
Poe's Tavern, 107
Sesame Burgers & Beer, 95
Vickery's Shem Creek Bar &
    Grill, 115

Savannah
Green Truck Neighborhood
    Pub, 178

Cafe

Charleston
East Bay Meeting House Bar &
    Cafe, 28
Gaulart & Maliclet, 30
181 Palmer, 73

Savannah
Clary's Cafe, 175
Gallery Espresso, 177

Chinese

Charleston
Dragon Palace Chinese Bistro, 104
Red Orchid's China Bistro, 138

Continental

Charleston
Dining Room at The Woodlands/
    The Pines, The, 96

Savannah
Noble Fare, 184

Crepes

Charleston
Tokyo Crepes, 130

Cuban

Charleston
El Bohio at The Pour House, 124

Appendix B: Index of Purveyors

Appendix C:
Index of Cooking Classes, Schools, Clubs & Forays

Appendix D: Index of Festivals & Events

Index